IT'S A GIRL'S LIFE IN THE ARMY!

BY GILLIAN WRIGHT

The author is a popular speaker at events all over the country. To book Gillian contact Jennie Storr at The Speakers Agency, jennie@thespeakersagency.com, 01522 522620/07809 063175

The following account is a true story as remembered by
the author. Names have been changed to protect the
innocent….

This book is dedicated to all Royal Green Jackets everywhere – no ordinary men, and to my husband – no ordinary man

Chapter One – The Idea

I never wanted to join the army. Not at all. I don't come from a military background in the Home Counties – more coalmining in North Notts and Derbyshire. My paternal grandfather was a rope-splicer at Langwith pit, my maternal grandmother picked potatoes for a halfpenny a row (I'm not sure how long the rows were), as her husband's nerves were too shot to bits to work much after his appalling experiences in the trenches during the First World War. And I'd never, ever, had any inclination to be physically fit. That was definitely for other people. People I didn't know, didn't have any connection with.

I lived and worked in London as a secretary-cum-researcher for a lovely old-fashioned company. But I had no prospects, I was bored and London was losing its appeal. I hadn't found the streets paved with gold, nor the man of my dreams.

"What to do?" I kept asking myself.

I was also getting very close to being Thirty Years Old, one of those landmarks when you start judging yourself.

"What have I achieved? Where am I going? I'm running out of time for the Big One? What is the Big One?" And it was then that I astonished myself by making a rather outrageous ,phone call.

It was January. Cold, wet, and for me miserable. Six months earlier I had found myself on my own yet again. This time it was me who had called the whole thing off, but that didn't make it any easier. Quite the reverse, it made it much harder. I now felt soiled, and branded as a let-down who couldn't be trusted, and I did feel a lot of guilt. The relationship had been getting very serious, about as serious as these things get. The date had been set. Church and reception were booked. Guest lists had been discussed at great length and eventually drawn up. My mother's beautiful lace wedding dress was in the process of being cut up and reshaped to fit my larger figure. Both sets of parents were excited and planning new outfits.

And I changed my mind. Irreversibly. And now there was the angst, at having let people down, at having wasted so much time and emotion on a man who was, in retrospect, so obviously not for me. (Nor me for him.) At having wasted his time and emotion. Our families' too. My beloved father, whom I had strived all my life to please and for whom I would have walked to Hell and back, had been so disgusted and disappointed at my letting everyone down that he told me he would never be able to trust me again.

I felt sliced raw by those words, confused and alone. I had tried, my God how I'd tried, to go through with it. I'd wrestled with my very identity in my effort to mould myself into that man's partner, trying to change myself to fit into what he'd wanted and I'd thought I ought to be. And then it had suddenly dawned on me that I didn't like what I was becoming and I was very afraid to look at myself or my future. I didn't like the way he made me feel. I just had to slam the brakes on. To react while there was just enough time. And now that the ear piercing screech of those brakes had gone resoundingly quiet, and the unpleasant debris had been picked over ad nauseam, I felt absolutely lost, very low with nothing to mould myself into anymore. I was frightened. It was like a long, slow silence. People I cared for deeply weren't talking to me. Memorably someone called me "fickle". And knowing, despite the apparent selfishness, right down in my heart that it had been the right thing to do to cancel the wedding - which my kinder and more loyal friends assured me it was - helped not a jot. I was scared at the emptiness of my life now and the emptiness of my future. I felt a Failure and I furtively carried around a heavy guilt like an unspeakable crime that needed to be paid for.

This was post-Christmas, post-New Year blues Big Time.

In a different frame of mind a few months earlier, I had seen an article about women being allowed to attend that previously all-male bastion the Royal Military Academy Sandhurst, for officer training, for the first time in its history. Of course, such a preposterous scenario was quite alien to me. The Army was a closed world upon which people like me did not even consider looking. I'd thought:

"How horrible, how ridiculous. And how and why and what sort of woman would do that............It would be worse than a prison sentence."

But what little seed had been embedded deeply, (unbeknown to me), in my subconscious by that strangely fascinating article? A prison sentence? A punishment?

So now, as I sat at my little desk in my office in Leicester Square that bleak, dank January day, thumbing through The Times, studying vacancies I suddenly saw it. "The Royal Military Academy Sandhurst is now seeking women for their September intake for officer training..........If you are interested telephone.........." and the number for the interested was that of a Colonel Plunkett-Smythe in Trafalgar Square. I jumped up, without thinking, to look out of the window.

"My God!" I thought, "I bet I can see his office from here." I scanned the wonderful view I had. There was Trafalgar Square. I squinted. Not sure of what I hoped to gain.   Then I tore my eyes from the window and grabbed the phone. Without a moment's hesitation I rang the number. Me! An office girl with her roots in a Nottinghamshire mining village.   I actually rang a Colonel Plunkett-Smythe about the September intake into Sandhurst! Had I gone quite mad?

I was breathing heavily into the mouthpiece. My heart thumping as I listened to the ringing tone. It seemed to go on for hours.   Then a kind, elderly, female voice thanked me for my call and in an unpromising tone assured me, in response to my stuttering enquiry, that the Colonel would return it when he was able. Ah, the thrill was over. Nothing had happened. A small element of relief. I returned heavily to the pile in my in-tray. Grey gloom crept insidiously back through the window. I was still the office girl.

About a week later I was having a really busy day. It was a Board Meeting day. The Chairman had arrived at about 8.30 that morning, and, only by extreme good luck, had managed to make his way upstairs to the Director General's office. He was very drunk, probably been drinking all night again, (so even handsome, rich, chauffeur-driven chairmen in immaculate bespoke suits and shiny cufflinks had Troubles). It was one hell of a job getting him sobered up for his appearance at the meeting by 10.30. I had to prepare endless cups of hot, sweet, black coffee, and rearrange all of the paperwork so that he would have only the briefest participation in the meeting. Just the merest of nods at a couple of vital moments, when sharply prodded. It was all systems go, and of course the telephone knew – as it always seems to – that this was a dodgy morning, and so persisted in ringing its head off.

"Hell-LO" I answered impatiently when it rang at a particularly tricky point, with the white-faced Chairman threatening to throw up all over his fabulous clothes.

"Hello, may I speak to Gillian Wright?" enquired a charming, and good-natured voice.

"Speaking", I snapped, moaning silently "Get on with it man, I haven't got all day."

"Can you talk?" enquired the smooth voice.

"Talk?" I thought, "Oh for Heaven's sake." And then aloud, "Go on."

"Well, could you get away and meet the Colonel some time today?"

Suddenly all thoughts of the poor Chairman looking very pale and about to throw up again, this time over the beautiful French-polished board table, went out of the window.

"Colonel?" I thought. "Colonel?" I'd completely forgotten my mad, impulsive, and really only half-serious call to the Sandhurst people. Who on earth was this?

"Yes," I whispered back, "yes," now completely bitten by the mystery and enthralled. My God, this was just what my life needed. What I longed for. An Adventure! Even if they had rung the wrong person I still wanted to grasp this opportunity whole-heartedly. My heart beat faster, I felt really alive. We arranged a visit for lunch-time that day. I was shaking with the sheer thrill and anticipation of it as I put down the phone.

Slowly, between urgent demands from the boardroom, I recalled the advert in the Times and my phone call. With memory came realisation; I was not Sandhurst material, I knew nothing of the Army, I was totally unfit and I had no idea of what I'd applied for. I was from the wrong background. And just how did one talk to a colonel? I'd really only been, well, filling in a boring half-hour in the office. Or had I? There was strangely something inside me that was determined I was going to make that meeting.

The hour drew near. I looked anxiously out of my little window across Leicester Square and in the direction of Trafalgar Square. The board meeting was over now, and a lengthy (probably very gloomy) post-mortem was now taking place in the DG"s office. All was very quiet. I slipped furtively out of my office and into the lift. There was a tangible air of unreality about it all. I was definitely playing a part.

I found the right place, it was an Army Recruiting Office. I'd passed it by millions of times without even noticing it. I'd never taken any interest. Now, however, I had a heightened interest in every detail. And I did notice that in asking for a lofty Colonel Plunkett-Smythe

I'd done something different to asking to see a lowly Private Smith.

I was directed up some stairs, and found myself standing in front of an unmarked door. It was some moments before I summoned enough courage to knock though, because I realised I'd no idea what on earth I was going to say when I entered. I also had no idea of what the outcome might be, unless it was to be told to stop wasting their time. Nevertheless, I knocked, a bit too loudly, at the door.

"Come," came the loud reply, and I came. It was a large, comfortable room, a beautiful room with a roaring log fire, large sofas, and it contained a very pleasant-looking man. Rather handsome. He had a large gin and tonic in one hand, and offered me one. Charming and disarming.

"Cheers," his smile was as warm as the fire. His very attractive eyes staring straight at me. I could feel myself slowly melting.

"Cheers," I responded, again a little too loudly, trying to sound like I always had G & Ts for lunch in such surroundings, and trying to control shaking hands. I suddenly felt very nervous. What the hell was I doing here?

"So," he paused, looking me straight in the eye. "You'd like to go to Sandhurst?"
I gulped audibly, aware that my right cheek was just beginning to twitch, but something came to the rescue. Probably the generous gin.

"Yes, I rather think I would." This time it came out far too quiet. So I cleared my throat, and said again more firmly, "Yes. I would."

"How do you keep fit, Miss Wright?"

"Fit?" I spluttered. I was stupid not to have been expecting this. My brain did a somersault. I took a large gulp of gin to give myself time and courage. What was a girl to say in such a situation? I was an office girl for goodness sake. I smoked – twenty a day, or more. My spare time was spent in Luciano and Giovanni's wine bar, just off Leicester Square, downing less than expensive wine. So I lied. Through my teeth. Like a Trooper. About how fit I was, about how I was naturally quite prepared to go for some weird-sounding pre-Sandhurst tests. I had to. There was simply no point telling the truth.

"Oh, quite. Quite. Absolutely......Gosh, yes. Very much so....." Gaining confidence now I kept on swigging his gin, repeating my assurances airily as though an old hand. After all, this wasn't quite Real Life was it? I could never go to Sandhurst. It was OK – I'd be out of here soon. Back to the office. None of it really mattered. And then it all seemed to flow quite naturally. I came out all smiles, holding a form for something called "Pre-RCB" – a first test that was to take place somewhere in about two months" time. Thus I floated, in a dreamlike state, out of the Army Recruiting Office and back into Trafalgar Square. And it all looked so very different.

Back at the office, the Boardroom now empty, (the suits having forensically picked over the morning's debacle), I sat down in front of my in-tray. Somehow the world had changed, and I was a different person from the one who had gone to Trafalgar Square a little over an hour ago. I had made a decision. I was on a Mission to be a new person, a fit person. And a girl who definitely didn't need a man getting in her way, messing up her future. And I certainly wasn't going to tell anyone….

Chapter Two – Getting Fit

I didn't come down from that cloud for two days. It was very nice up there. My whole life seemed to have taken on a new hue. I felt cheerful, no problem was too great, no-one's manners too objectionable. The weather became irrelevant. I no longer looked at happy couples and envied them. Well, maybe I did a bit. But I had other things on my mind now. My mission became my companion, and it kept me secretly warm inside.

This was Life, and somehow I was Living it again. Having an Adventure. My own private little adventure. I had told no-one about my trip to Trafalgar Square because I was perfectly aware that it would have resulted in complete and absolute horror, ridicule and disbelief on the part of any of my friends, family and even acquaintances. After all, wasn't I fickle, untrustworthy? Such reaction would have shot down my cloud like a stone. I would have clearly seen that applying to Sandhurst was not only ridiculous, but also was not going to happen. I was never going to go all the way with this. I would Fail before I got anywhere close. But, for a couple of days I wanted my little cloud to keep floating above the humdrum of cold, dark, miserable winter days in my little office.

Eventually I braved studying the form to apply for the pre-RCB test. I'd hidden it in my bedroom at the house I shared with friends in Balham. It was a long form, but not too difficult to complete. There was also a lot of additional information to read. All about Sandhurst, and the pre-Sandhurst interviews and tests. I read secretly in my room about a world that was utterly different to anything I had experienced before. A world that was completely closed off to me. I slowly felt the warm glow of a secret challenge beginning to creep over me. The Army was tough wasn't it? Punishingly tough? I could pay for my crimes. And along the way I might excel, be brave. Maybe even make my beloved father proud again. I'd damn well show them! I was excited. Very excited.

But what about reality? I had lied my head off, well, certainly bluffed. I was not fit. I spent my spare time smoking and drinking with my friends, (in Giovanni's and Luciano's snug and welcoming little wine bar just off Leicester Square). I had never possessed trainers (nor jogging kit). In my wildest dreams I'd never thought of going jogging. I had swum occasionally. I could even recall going horse-trekking once, on holiday in North Wales, but I'd been about seven and the horse only managed an arthritic amble – about my level really. And then we'd found out I was allergic to horses and I sneezed violently for the whole day.

So, how on earth did I think I was going to do this? I looked at the form again: the pre-Regular Commissioning Board test was taking place in two months' time, in Camberley. Where the hell was Camberley? I looked at the pictures, of men and women doing unspeakable things in mud, up walls, through cold rivers. No doubt about it, some form of preparation was going to be necessary. But how did a drinking, smoking, over-weight office girl prepare in secret ? For that?

I didn't post the application locally, but sent it from a little box in central London – just in case anyone should see me and say, "Hey, what are you doing applying to Sandhurst, you mad or what?" I kept putting my hand in the letterbox to make absolutely certain that it wasn't stuck half-way down. My whole life now seemed to depend on that form making it to its destination.

I visited Marks and Sparks to see if they did such things as trainers. They did, and furtively I tried a pair on. They felt very strange and I left the store quickly, all embarrassed, and it took yet another trip to actually buy the things. Then I realised I only had two months, so I quickly purchased a pair of track suit bottoms and a sweat shirt as well. I tried them on in my room back home, and I began to feel the part. I had the kit. Now I'd see if that made it possible for me to run. I became very interested in the movements of the others in the house, finding out which evening they'd all be out, and I excused myself from the wine bar. I was on a positive high by the time I'd got myself dressed up and ready to go. I crept down to the hall, and stood by the front door.

"No, I can't," I said out loud. "I can't go out like this. And pretend to run. What if someone sees me?" Gently I cajoled myself,

"Just start by walking and see how you feel. Just pretend you always dress like this to jog to the shops, and if you feel like breaking into a trot whilst humming a little tune, well, if that comforts you just do it."

14

Stepping, gingerly, into the street I walked a bit. Then I actually speeded up until I almost jogged. My feet thumped the pavement, I could feel my backside wobble, and then my heart felt like it was going to burst. After five minutes, my lungs were gasping, great wheezes were erupting, my face was puce, and my knees began to tremble and buckle. How far had I gone? About six lamp-posts" worth.

It took me a while to stagger back to the house, all fears of being seen wiped out by now fearing for my very survival. (Once in the house it must have taken an hour for my poor body to consider surviving again). After an hour and a half the trembling began to subside. The doorbell rang, and in came my friend Iain.

"Gilli, darling, whatever's happened? You look dreadful? Do you need a drink? Here, have one of mine." He offered his open cigarette packet. I stared at it. I was glad I'd already ripped off the trainers and hidden them. I made some feeble excuse about having done the vacuuming too vigorously. I hastily excused myself and with that I fled to my room. Phew! Close shave.

And there were still only two months for a miracle to take place.

Next day, when I woke up, I could hardly move. My chest ached terribly, my legs felt sore. Getting my feet into my tights was an effort; getting to the tube station was horrible; sitting down in my chair at my desk was painful. Everyone kept asking me what was wrong. Why did my face contort when I reached for the keyboard; why did I wince and sigh deeply every two minutes? I invented a draught. A strong, cold draught. That I'd had to sit in for simply ages last night at

15

Somebody's house. It'd made me stiff. That seemed to keep everyone happy for a bit.

I had to have a new plan. I couldn't face that jogging again. Not for a while anyway. There was a swimming pool nearby, that might be a better start. I bought a swimming costume and set to. A few lengths were quite enough to begin with, and gradually I built up – a length at a time.

A month had flown by when a brown envelope addressed to me "On Her Majesty's Service" landed on the mat. The envelope contained detailed instructions about my forthcoming pre-RCB tests. As I read it through in the privacy of my little room I could hear my heavy breathing and my heart thumping. I'd got to get myself to Camberley, in Surrey, where I would be collected, and taken on. I would need to take 3 days off work. There were three weeks left. I wondered if I should try the jogging again.

Chapter 3 – The First Test

The day before my departure to Camberley I told everyone I was spending a few days with some fictitious friends. My small bag had already been packed for at least a week but, each evening, I feverishly checked its contents to be sure I'd not forgotten anything vital. It didn't help that I didn't know what was vital. It was guess work. But I was fitter than I had ever been before; I could now jog around the whole block fairly comfortably, and still manage 20 a day.   I was rather pleased with myself.

I'd never been to Surrey before, but the journey down wasn't arduous . I was nervous but excited. This was a Real Adventure. No-one knew where I was, nor what I was up to. It was a great feeling of liberation, especially as none of it seemed particularly real.   When the train stopped at Camberley, several rather smart-looking girls got out, and we made our way over to a female soldier holding a clipboard.   She read off our names, and we climbed on board a white minibus.   No-one uttered a word. I started to feel a bit sick. Gradually one or two asked the usual sort of, "Where have you come from?" questions, but nothing more.   The air hung with a nervous anticipation.   I realised that I was probably by far the oldest, but I hadn't worked out, yet, that I was also definitely the greenest.

Once the bus stopped at what was to be our base for the next two and a half days, another female soldier suddenly appeared from nowhere and broke out into some extraordinary, extremely loud, barking.   I froze with shock. Mouth open and staring. Had she suddenly been taken ill?   But apparently we were being commanded to march.   I immediately dropped my handbag, and was shrieked at. Very red in the face and extremely flustered I tried to grab the bag and fall in with the rest. I was totally, utterly and absolutely out of place.   Clueless. By the time we'd "marched" across what seemed to be a great big field, and into some horrid little huts I was exhausted. In a state of shock I reached for my cigarettes.

"There's no smoking in here," whispered another girl. Adventure? What was I doing?

I thought that, after our journey we wouldn't be asked

to do anything until the next day. I certainly needed to rest. Wrong. We were shouted at, screamed at, marched here, there and everywhere until late in the evening. We were given half an hour to grab something from what they called the "cookhouse", and taken into a field to be given our "Command Tasks" whilst there was still a shred of light.

It was cold. I didn't understand the instructions. I wasn't sure how to take command, but some of the girls did take charge and started telling the rest of us what to do. I felt miserable as I simply couldn't get my head around any of it. I knew I was being inadequate. My fragile daydream began to crumble, and my confidence with it. I was nearly thirty. I'd no career, my love life was a barren desolate wasteland, my family were ashamed of me, and now this. I'd set myself up for a major failure - again.

I guess I was on the rebound. I think, in my still guilt-ridden state, I'd thought applying for the Army would take away the pain and the guilt of having finished with someone who, despite being wrong for me, had loved me, I think. He'd planned to marry me. I'd let him down, I'd let my parents down. His too. Everyone had been so shocked I'd ended it. No-one dared to talk about it, even me, there was so much hurt surrounding it. I was full of conflicting, confusing feelings. Should I have gone ahead and married him despite all of my misgivings? Should I just have kept everyone happy? Made my wonderful father proud at the Posh "Do" he would have had to save so hard for, longed for, and could have shown off at?

I guess I'd thought that applying for the Army would give me a different goal. I could make a new life for myself, a new identity. Maybe I could be proud of myself. Maybe I could provide a different reason for my father to be proud of me. I was struggling find a solution, a meaning out of the mess I felt I'd created. Going to Sandhurst would also provide me with a different pain, a physical punishment which could help me to pay for my "crime".

It had appeared a perfect solution. This was not an affair on the rebound. It was a whole new life, away from the family. New friends would emerge who knew nothing of my deed. It would be a physically gruelling test to assuage my guilt. In all an opportunity to prove myself, and win back some pride. Perfect.

But hang on, I was a complete idiot. It was on the rebound even if it wasn't an affair. It was never going to work. I just wasn't capable. I was making a fool of myself. I felt utterly miserable. And with that my dark little cloud shed its rain.

At last, we were told that we could get a hot drink from the cookhouse. Nothing better than a cup of tea after a bit of inner turmoil! We could then retire to our huts, but we were told to be back outside, lined up at 6 am for breakfast. I felt terribly tired, terribly cold and terribly disappointed. It was true to say I hurt. All over.

But back in the huts, the lights were on. It felt warm. The other girls started to become real people, the chatting was more friendly now, as a group. We were in it together. I was no threat to anyone as no-one, I realised, was as unprepared or as ill-equipped as me.

The other girls were astonished at my grand age of 28. Their average age being about 20. They obviously thought me rather odd not to be married off by now, let alone wanting to embark on this lark. I kept stum and I learned a lot that evening. I listened intently to a corporal who desperately wanted to get to Sandhurst and become an officer. She explained about command tasks and, slowly, I began to understand the point of them. Another, who had been in the University Cadet Force, explained other tests that we would undoubtedly be faced with the next day. Everyone was terribly helpful and, although exhausted, at least I knew that I wouldn't freeze with shock when someone barked at me now. I was a little better prepared, and wanted to go on with it. I sneaked out for a quick fag, and gave myself a bit of a pep talk under the stars.

The next day I threw myself into my attempt to get through the tests. I struggled to look reasonably intelligent, resilient and fit. And, with the strangeness of it all my enthusiasm returned. I really wanted to do something so very, very different so very, very much. There were two more days of basic fitness tests, command tasks, and discussion groups which were watched over by the eagle eyes of the examiners, scribbling every time anyone so much as twitched. And at the end of it all we were given the results – would we be invited back for the next round, the RCB, or would we be told that we had reached the end of this particular road?

We lined up outside a room, and waited anxiously for our turn to be called in. Everyone wanted to go on to the next stage, everyone was stony quiet as we waited. But I, perhaps more than others, was desperate not to fail. Something inside me had been all lit up. I was itching to continue with this mad adventure. It was desperately important to achieve this to fill a gap in my life, a gap I felt so keenly. I'd missed my chance of married security. Doomed now to be an eternal gooseberry, I wanted to achieve this for myself, by myself. It was a light, bright and shining, at the end of my dark tunnel.

When I was called in, the faces looked at me kindly. Oh dear. Probably not a good sign. I was told that my fitness, or lack of it, had let me down. I was told that I hadn't really seemed to grasp the command tasks. I was told that I was, perhaps, a little too old. At this my lip began to tremble, my eyes began to fill up. "And too old for what else?" I began to think miserably. And then I was asked for my view.

I've no recall of exactly what I said, but I do know I felt as though I'd lived a whole new life in that two and a half days. I'd found myself again. It had been wonderful, invaluable, and yes of course I wanted to go on. Fervently. My words seemed to hang in the air, and I waited in the stillness whilst there was a little conferring. I was told I was borderline, but, if I managed to improve my fitness, and work on my command tasks then I might stand a chance at the RCB.

"Could you, Miss Wright, improve on your fitness?"

"Oh Absolutely," I gushed imploringly. "Yes, I agree I need to, and I most certainly could." Complete bluff of course, I'd have promised anything. In truth I was at a loss as to how on earth I could do more fitness training than I already had done, I was fitter than I had ever been in my entire life. After all, I had been thrilled to stagger round the whole block – more than 50 lamp-posts worth!

They smiled, I thought at my correct answer.

"And do you think Miss Wright, that you could improve on your command tasks?"

"Oh yes, Absolutely. Absolutely." Inside silently, "how on earth do they think I can possibly do that? I still don't have a clue what a command task is and, as I've never bumped into one in Balham, nor in Giovanni's and Luciano's wine bar, what chance do I have to brush up on one?" However, still determined at this desperate moment I gave it my all, agreeing and saying "Absolutely" to absolutely everything they asked.

And so, remarkably, I was invited to apply for the next stage. I managed to thank them, and then get out of the room before bursting into tears. It was a wonderful moment, full of promise once more.

I felt Great.

Something that had been started back in Leicester Square as only half-serious had now become the most serious thing in my life. No-one else knew it, but I was now more than determined to become an officer in Her Majesty's Forces, an Army officer.

Back in Balham the house was quiet, it was quite late at night, and there was no-one to ask me if I'd enjoyed my stay with my fictitious friends. I had a quiet smoke in the lounge, musing over the last few days. I needed a drink and poured a stiff one. Tomorrow I'd work out a proper fitness programme, but tonight I was just going to enjoy being one real step further on. Oh yes, life as a single woman could be just as fulfilling. Just as rewarding. I might be down but I wasn't Out. Oh no, not yet.

Chapter 4 – The Next Test

Next day in the office I should have felt tired. But I didn't. I was on top of the world. Still no-one knew of my eccentric and outrageous venture, so I felt like I was living a secret double life. Everyone wanted to know if I'd had a nice break, and then it was as if nothing had happened – for them. For me, I was embarking on a whole new life. Now I'd got to research how to improve my fitness.

Making a great start I wandered around Covent Garden at lunch-time, indulging in the wickedest creations I could spot in the sandwich bars. What the hell? I felt like I deserved it, and I'd sure as hell burn off the calories on my new fitness regime. However, what this new regime actually would be was anyone's guess. Dawdling around – more my style – I spotted a poster on a lamppost. It read "The Pineapple Dance Studio...........Aerobics, Tap, Ballet................"

"Wow", I thought. "That sounds more fun, and definitely more glamorous than counting lampposts in Balham." It occurred to me that a positive benefit of aerobics at the Pineapple Dance Studio was that I might actually brave admitting to friends and relations where I was going. All this sneaking out to jog at the oddest hours to avoid recognition was becoming a bit of a strain. Thus decided, I made enquiries that very evening.

Another new outfit. This time leotard and leggings. At least the trainers could still be used. The downside of the new kit was that it was less kind than baggy tracksuit and sweatshirts. Spare bits popped out and wobbled in unflattering places. It actually didn't hide any of my sins, no matter how hard I tried to stretch various bits of the leotard over them.

However, I was on a mission, and I was giving it my best shot – even if it did mean humiliation in shedloads along the way.

I'd never thought of myself as having a good figure, simply because I'd never had one. It certainly affected my confidence with the opposite sex.   I felt it had detracted from my ability to attract. It was odd then that, now I was embarking on getting fit, and hopefully a trimmer figure, I had given up wanting a man.   I was doing this for me.

My first venture into aerobics land is lodged in my memory. For ever.   I was useless; an uncoordinated lump of torso and limbs.   Bits of me that weren't supposed to be there enthusiastically joining in, but woefully out of time to the music. After the first five minutes of "warming up" I was almost exhausted with a face like a radish newly plucked from the ground. But, despite this, I rather liked it. It felt glamorous to be in a real dance studio – I'd never had the nerve, nor the inclination, to approach one before. The music was fast and fun. I started to tell people where I was going. And their response was rather gratifying.

"Really? Gosh. You are good."   No-one laughed. Apart from my sister, of course.

In time, progress was made – a good job, as the date for the RCB test was approaching quickly. I didn't reach complete exhaustion until near the end of the sessions now.   I'd also given up counting lampposts, and could now concentrate on jogging around whole blocks. The swimming was helping too. But it was becoming difficult to explain my absences from parties and the wine bar. It was also difficult explaining why I was hanging around the house, hovering expectantly, ushering people out of the front door, so I could get my kit on, do a quick few blocks and get back before anyone else returned. I don't really know now how I managed to keep it all up.

The day the letter came, headed "The Regular Commissioning Board", and giving me detailed instructions on reporting to Westbury in Wiltshire, I had my first real doubts. These were Big Doubts, the sort that make you think there is a real chance that you need help from those men in white coats. There was no excitement this time, just a slightly jippy tummy, and a complete lack of concentration on work and social life. Even when I tried to jog or do aerobics there was no puff, no fizz, no drive – except to dash to the lavatory.

I was panicking.

"What on earth do you think you are doing? No wonder you haven't told anyone, it's madness, and you don't really want to do this do you? Not really. You were just trying to escape from something- real life. This is a pipe dream. You can't really do it. You should have got married. You should just hide in a hole."

This just went round and round my head all day, and what was worse all night.

I went out one evening with a friend, someone I thought of as a sort of close cousin. We'd been friends for years, and he was a good laugh but intelligent and could be sensible too. I liked him a great deal. I could talk to him if he was in the right mood, so I thought I might try broaching The Subject for the very first time. Just to test the water. It might help me re-enthuse myself. After a few for dutch courage, I tentatively began by telling him, truthfully, that I'd met someone who was in the Army and it sounded a great life...?? I waited to see his reaction.

"Mmm, really. I would have thought it was Hell," mused my chum Adrian.

"No, no." I responded, "It all sounded terribly interesting and exciting too. They seemed to really enjoy it," I pushed on desperately hoping to hear something helpful.

"Must be mad," he stated baldly. I changed the subject, a little unnerved, deflated. He was right wasn't he?

Westbury. It sounded an important place. Far away. Again, somewhere I'd never been. More fictitious friends – different ones this time. Three days booked off work. Bag packed, train ticket purchased and nerves. Great big jangly ones. I didn't enjoy the journey down. My mind was somewhere else. My stomach sickly, its contents constantly coming up into my throat.

"Could you, do you think Miss Wright, improve on your fitness?" "Oh yes. Absolutely." And, "Could you, Miss Wright, improve your command tasks?" ....Oops. Still didn't really know what that one was. How was I to know if what I had done was enough? I was so ignorant.

I arrived at Westbury railway station along with the rest of the hopefuls. This time our programme for the next three days was explained to us at the start and I was devastated when I realised I would have to sit examination papers, including maths. All hope drained out of me.

At school my maths teacher had refused to put me in for maths O level saying it would be a "waste of time and public money," even the lesser qualification, the CSE, had defeated me. So, after all that, I was going to fail anyway. My mother always said I'd regret not trying harder at bloody maths. Should I tell someone straightaway that there was no point? I felt unsure. Gloom descended, and I barely heard what else we'd got to do.

I decided to crack on, and was absolutely delighted to see that I could keep up with the fitness tests. That felt great, and I was more heartened. If I failed to get in now at least I could hold on to that small but, for me, enormous achievement.

The command tasks were dodgy, but I tried to take charge and command my team with confidence to build a raft out of two twigs and a filthy oil drum, and to sail it down a freezing river and over a rapid with good humour and, almost, complete safety.

The discussion groups didn't daunt me either – I always had a lot to say on any subject you liked, but I expected that it was just as important to listen too. In other words, I had more of a feel for where the points could be notched up.

There was only one girl there who I'd met at the pre-RCB, she was very pleasant as were most of the others. We all started to share our nerves, our concerns and our hopes, and it was interesting to see how quickly we began to feel close to each other during these testing three days. The officers and soldiers who surrounded us with clipboards seemed a decent lot too, even if they did shout and scream for most of the day and night, and didn't give us enough time to get a satisfying and much-hungered for meal.

There was a wonderful colour sergeant on the directing staff. He was Scottish, approachable, with a fantastic sense of humour. He was fair, and oozed empathy. It didn't take more than five minutes for me to feel an enormous sense of respect and liking for this man. When it turned out that this wonderful colour sergeant was to be the invigilator for our examinations I poured my heart out to him.

"There's no point in me doing the maths exam." I told him. "Quite simply I can't do maths." He went over to his desk and took out a big file of papers.

"I see from your application forms," he said "that you haven't recorded any qualification in maths."

"No" I replied glumly, "I don't have any."

"Well, have a go," he insisted, "You never know, you might find it's not as bad as you expect, and you don't have to do it all. Just have a shot at the first few questions, take your time, and don't worry about it. You only need to do the first few which are easier than the later ones."

With his encouraging smiles and nods throughout the next hour or so, I did my best. I didn't want to let him down, or let myself down. When it came to the allotted hour to put our pens down, he gave me a bit of extra time, not much, but enough for me to remember his kindness for ever.

It was a relief to get that exam over with and the kindness and support shown to me really did spur me on.

I wanted to belong to the same army that that colour sergeant belonged to. The next day or so felt somehow better, knowing that I'd been supported, and respected, despite my deficiency.   When someone shouted commands at me I knew that underneath there was a real person, a very decent person.   It made it all so much easier.

At this final stage as it were, it all being much more serious, complex too I suppose, we wouldn't hear whether we'd got through for six weeks.   References were going to be looked into. This seemed appropriate. After all it wasn't just a question of "getting through", it was a question of whether or not we'd been accepted for a coveted place at the world's most elite military training establishment, The Royal Military Academy Sandhurst.

As I journeyed home I thought of all my friends and relations. Just what would they say if I were?

Chapter 5 – The Result

Work was busy as usual. It was now not just the poor Chairman who had a drink problem, but also the DG's new PA, who had found the responsibility for holding the key to the private drinks cupboard just too tempting. Glenda had become a real pal to me.   I loved her eccentricities, her loud stage voice, and the fact that when her front tooth had broken on her breakfast toast one morning she was only half an hour late, breezily announcing with a light lisp, as she sailed into the office, that she'd stuck it back into place with Araldite glue. She was just wonderful, very theatrical and, as we shared an office, we laughed our way through most eventualities most days.

My thoughts of RCBs and Sandhurst became less real as the weeks passed. It didn't seem very likely now that it could happen and life had gone on, more or less, as it had always done.

One day Glenda and I were told by the DG that we were to have a trade delegation visiting from Japan. The DG really wanted to put on a show. Arrangements were to be detailed, comprehensive, and impressive. Glenda and I were put in charge of making all the arrangements, and as a reward, we were very kindly asked to attend the final event – a grand, formal dinner to be held at the DG"s Pall Mall Gentleman's club. All very exciting.

However, no women were allowed into this club, except on special occasions, and only then if a room was privately hired. Presumably the old buffers in there would go into a dead faint if they spotted a female in the public areas? Would we have to wear paper bags over our tantalising forms until we got into the private room?

The visit itself went really well. We'd all worked terribly hard, and at last the final evening's dinner was looming. Glenda and I had both bought new dresses, and I must admit that even I, knowing Glenda well, took a double take at the outfit she had chosen It was quite extraordinary in its grandness and was to be topped off with a rather magnificent blonde wig. I was somewhat taken aback at this new departure, she looked so different, so...........very different. However, we both assured each other that we looked "Lovely. Really. Smashing. No Really." And we set off in a taxi for the very smart, very stuffy, exclusively all male club, where we had hired a private room. (Thank God.)

The DG was in fine, expansive form, and the Japanese seemed to be having a whale of a time. I was completely fascinated by how much wine they could drink, and it certainly seemed to be flowing. Talking of which, this was a poignant and very defining event in my life. One that introduced me to one of Life's great pleasures – brandy. I recall berating my father the next evening on the telephone for not introducing me to brandy earlier in my life – I'd missed years of this wondrous pleasure, and the truly tremendous effects it might have had.

It was only after everyone else had left the dinner party that the rather shocking view of Glenda's body slurred into my vision. She was lying, inert, over 3 chairs, her head lolling off the end of one of them. Her magnificent wig having rolled across the room. It occurred to me that I wasn't sure how long she'd lain like that, or if anyone else had noticed her condition. I inexpertly sat her up, and stuffed her wig into my handbag. I called a waiter for black coffee, and water.

Although she revived enough to say, "hullo Geelly," and giggle, she was obviously in no fit state to go home by train to Kent. Or by any other means. The brandy having made me brilliant, and more dangerously having persuaded me that I was indeed brilliant, a great idea struck me. The DG kept a bedroom on at his club. Just in case he needed to stay over in central London sometimes. I knew he wasn't using it that night. I explained to the club staff, in my most imperious manner, that we needed the key to the DG"s room as he'd asked us to store some very important papers there after the dinner. There seemed to be no problem. The staff were most obliging. It only remained for me to haul Glenda up the stairs and into the room, and to hope that when she woke up in the

31

morning she would manage to get out without anyone seeing her.

It all seemed to work a treat. I deposited Glenda, in the recovery position, and made my way home happy in the knowledge that I'd pulled off a blinder. However, when Glenda arrived at work the next morning, looking like death warmed up only a little bit, we didn't dare to breathe a word about any of it. The DG never mentioned it either. I've no idea if anyone ever found out about it. But sadly Glenda didn't last much longer at the company. Her forays into the drinks cabinet proved her downfall in the end. I'd love to see that wonderful woman again.

One evening my father telephoned me to say he was coming down to London the following week, and "Let's make a go of it." It was great to see him. He was painfully aware of my general dissatisfaction and discomfort with life/career/universe etc. and had always been a good shoulder to cry on when work was getting me down, when my failing relationships became truly failed, or life was just becoming meaningless. Although I was painfully aware that he'd been a bit distant since my major fiasco. He asked how my job hunting was going.

"Found anything yet?"

I was desperate to tell someone, and here I was with my dear old dad, friend and often erstwhile counsellor. If there was anyone I wanted to share The Secret with it was him. I wanted to make up for so much and somehow I felt it was the right moment to share it. However, after all that had happened, all that had been said, I wasn't sure how my news would be received. I took a deep breath and eased myself in.

"Yes. I have. Well, not exactly a job really. But yes,

I have found something I want to do." He looked interested.

"Not exactly a job eh?" he queried. "Then what? Not more fees for education?"

I wanted to spin it out, and challenged him,

"You've got to guess. Go on."

He entered the spirit of the challenge but, of course, he never came anywhere near the truth. Not within a million miles.

"I give up," he admitted.

I took a deep breath,

"Really want to know? Really, really?"

"Of course," he replied, beginning to look a bit weary.

I took a deeper breath. This was my big secret about to receive its first airing.

"I've applied to join the Army. To go to Sandhurst."

I don't know how I'd expected my father to respond to this frankly astonishing announcement but there was no reaction, he just stared at me. I started to feel anxious. I'd not pleased him? He was disappointed in me again? He didn't believe me?

"I mean it," I said imploring a response. "I really have. I've been for tests and everything. And interviews and all sorts over the last few months." Still no response, then suddenly, and a little strangled,

"The Army?"

"Yes," I shouted out. His body began to shake, he went red in the face, his mouth opened, and out they came, big belly laughs. They got bigger with every breath he took. I was embarrassed. Everyone was looking at us. My father looked as though he would fall off his chair and damage himself. He was helpless. I'd never seen him laugh like that before.

I decided not to tell anyone else about my secret after that. I was glad I'd got it off my chest to someone and glad it was my father, but I wasn't sure he took it at all seriously, even after I'd given him time for it to sink in. However, I knew to the day when the expected letter from the Regular Commissions Board was due and, as I'd asked for it to be sent to my parents' house, I took some holiday to be sure I was there when it arrived. I had never been so nervous in my life. I had never wanted anything so much in all my life. A couple of days before the due day I decided to tell my mother all about it – I wanted her to know and I wanted her to be there when I opened the letter. She wept openly. She wondered where she had gone wrong. Why had her youngest daughter decided to do anything so terrible? How could I possibly contemplate wearing those boots?

She continued to weep over the next couple of days but did nothing to dent my resolve. I wanted, more than wanted, to go to Sandhurst. This was It. Not a wedding, but something better in the end. Something I knew I wanted, for me. Not for anyone else. The day arrived. It was a Saturday and I got up terribly early. My parents' postwoman didn't come to the house until around eleven in the morning so I decided to go for a run. A run! Was this how I was going to react to stress from now on? Not the usual fag and black coffee? I had to admit that the novelty of feeling physically fit was worth experiencing. I felt bright, alert, ready for anything and much less tired. The effect was uplifting physically and mentally and quite different from feeling a sluggard. I wanted to remember how good it felt, I wanted to remember how it had been worth achieving. I didn't want to lose it, whatever happened next.

Whilst I ran my mind was racing too. How would I feel if I'd failed to gain a place? How would I feel if I'd got a place? What would the Sandhurst people be like? I'd be so much older. Would that matter? Would people question my sexual orientation, being older and single? Would that matter? Would I fit in? How tough would it be? What would it be like to go back to the old routine if I'd failed to win a place? Would I still try to keep fit or would I symbolically throw my trainers away and die an old maid who felt she'd achieved nothing? Would I be able to cope with the anti-climax?

The run couldn't last forever, and eventually I arrived back at my parents" house. Still only 8 o'clock. I tried to eat breakfast. It was like dust. I mooched around. I rang a friend and talked about nothing. When 11 o'clock came, and the postwoman didn't, I started to fidget and jump up and down, my anxiety straining all tolerance levels. And then she came, down the gravelled path, crunch, crunch. The post dropped, loudly, onto the front mat. All went deadly quiet. Still. I ran and picked up the brown envelope. The, by now familiar, "On Her Majesty's Service" printed boldly. I couldn't tell from the look, or the feel, of the envelope whether it was going to say "yes", or "no". My fingers trembled. I ran into the kitchen where my mother was trying to stay calm and tactful.

"Mum you open it. Please. I can't." I said weakly.

"Are you sure? Of course I will, if you really want me to." I nodded, not wanting to breathe let alone speak. If I prayed now would it help? Or had the die been cast? She opened it and, without looking, passed it to me, tactful to the end.

"Please read it too," I asked dully. She took a deep breath.

"Dear Gillian," she began as I tried to be patient, "Following your recent interviews for................" I nearly burst.   Then I heard the never to be forgotten words, "And has pleasure in offering you a place for the Sandhurst intake 861 for January 1986."

The world stopped.   I gasped.   And then burst into tears. We both cried. Then I wondered if I'd misheard.

"Read it again, quick," I shouted, and she did.   We cried again.   Then we rushed down to the bottom of the garden where my father was also tactfully busying himself, polishing the fence posts.   He gave me a huge hug, and we all cried, together.

Chapter 6 – So now you know

I was dying to tell everyone, and it was the greatest fun.   The shocked disbelief on the faces of friends, who hadn't even known I'd bought that pair of trainers, let alone run in them, was terrific.   It was like the greatest practical joke I'd ever played.   My sister was so shocked she simply didn't know what to say, or how to react. After the shock receded, most were terribly proud of me, curious, and rather excited.   This was September, and I had 3 or 4 months to prepare myself.   More seriously now.

It was harder to explain to people at work who obviously thought I was mad.   My much-loved boss, Harold, was genuinely choked as I told him I'd be leaving, which I hadn't expected.   However, in his sensible Lancashire tones, he declared,

"Three-and-a- half years isn't long lass, and ye can

cum back." It was a small company, a hundred people, and I knew them all, so it wasn't long before everyone knew I was leaving, and why. They were all very supportive and that support came in handy.

I continued to train, only much harder. Realising that I would be a bit older than most of the other women I had a real fear that I might be left behind on runs. So my training programme, made so much easier now it was all out in the open, was stepped up. I ran every day before breakfast and the Pineapple Dance Studio got sick of seeing me. Then one horrible day, whilst doing aerobics, I twisted my ankle. It was a very bad twist. Instead of being sensible and resting I thought, "I'm fit, it'll be OK," and I tried to battle on. The ankle got worse, much worse. One day, walking around Soho, it collapsed beneath me and I fell off the kerb into the road. The motorist managed to avoid me but I ended up in Casualty in a lot of pain.

I was referred to physiotherapy. I was desperate. Only two months to go, and I could hardly walk. The physiotherapist was great, kind and sympathetic, but still she uttered cruel words.

"There is no way you can contemplate joining the Army in January, your ankle is simply never going to be able to take the strain."

I was miserable but the Director General went into fatherly mode. He sent me along to his osteopath, paying himself for as many sessions as might help while his new Personal Assistant recommended a teacher of the Alexander Technique. The physiotherapist continued to work overtime and I did everything they all advised. It kept me busier than ever. Christmas was coming but I never contemplated contacting the Army and telling them I wasn't going to make it. Rather I scoured the local chemist for sprays that would help me kill the pain in my ankle.

It did get a lot better and, as the office closed for Christmas, there were many good-byes to say. I didn't find it easy. I was saying good-bye to my life for the past 6 years, and to a lot of wonderful friends. Even the Receptionist at work, someone who had been my friend, confidante, and provider of much information, (she was also everyone else's confidante), bought me a gift. A towel with "Hair" written on it, and some shampoo for my showers after long runs. Everyone was so kind, but leaving also felt great. I'd had enough of living in digs in London. I longed for fields again. A fresh start. Life had held a few disappointments and, every time I thought back to that day I made the phone call to the colonel in Trafalgar Square, I knew absolutely that I wanted, needed, to move on.

That Christmas was a happy one. I felt fulfilled and full of excitement. I couldn't help noticing that my sister's boyfriend „phoned her every morning and every evening while we were with my parents. Yes, I envied her the closeness of their warm relationship, but I could accept that it hadn't happened for me. I still felt the pain and the guilt but I had something else to cling on to now, to put my energy into.

In a way I wanted that Christmas to last forever, it was wonderful to have so much to look forward to, even though I was very nervous. But, as with all things one wants to last, Christmas sped by. I was busy packing, according to the long list supplied to me and trying to think what little luxuries I might soon be grateful for. We were allowed to take our own duvet, a cassette player and radio. We could also take things to decorate our room with, and photo's. Even with the list to help, packing was a never-ending chore. I was adding something to my cases every half-hour "just in case".

Then that much-thought-about day arrived. My parents were to drive me down to Sandhurst and stay with me for a short time to see the accommodation. Then they would leave and Army Life would begin. We were all nervous. My father had served for a few years in the Navy during the war, and couldn't resist recounting rotten stories about regimental life, and always ended up reminding me that no-one in the world was less regimented than his daughter.

"I hope you'll be able to keep your room tidy," he kept repeating helpfully, with a nervous chuckle.

Then, there it was; the grand entrance, big gates and long drive sweeping away. Soldiers were on guard. I don't know what I'd expected, but this looked like Buckingham Palace to me. I suddenly thought of all the illustrious people who had come here before me: my hero David Niven had spent three years here, (the officer training course was longer in those days); our royal family, the Sultan of Oman, King Hussein of Jordan, (whose daughter, Princess Aiysha, was at Sandhurst right now, on the course above me)...... and so on. We got out of the car and explained who we were, were given a pass and directed up the drive. By now I was feeling rather sick. When I first saw Old College immaculate, sparkling white, and reflected in the beautiful lake, very majestic, I did think "Wow." We parked near the all-hallowed Old College parade square, and I stared at it wondering if people really marched on it, in those impressive surroundings. Then we went to see the not-so-impressive room where I would live. Bare. Basic. Cold-looking. Iron bedstead. Lots of nervous, smart girls with lots of nervous, smart parents.

Someone in charge politely told the parents to leave, and I tried to hold on, tight, to mine.

"Don't forget," said my father, "I'll be waiting for the call. Just ring as soon as you get fed up with it and I'll come to get you straight away." Well, he probably knew me better than anyone.

"Right." I replied. "I won't forget." And silently, "That'll get me through this if nothing else will. Don't think I can hack it eh?" Then they'd gone. The sickness came back but I was given no time at all to think about it as we were herded off to a large hall.

The male intake was gathered there with us, and I was astounded how many of them were there. About 800. And only about 50 of us females. We were ordered to be silent and to watch a video displayed on a big screen with the volume turned up as high as it might go. What I saw shocked me dreadfully, it was all about the dangers of fire whilst on military duty, about using live and loud ammunition. Soldiers getting dreadfully burnt in a petrol accident. Fires starting in woods on exercise and explosions going horribly wrong. It was sickeningly shocking and I guess it was meant to be. At the end we were ordered out and lined up, men separate from the women. I was still trembling when a female soldier came and shouted at us to march to the cookhouse for tea. We did, in deadly silence. Not one of us feeling in the least bit hungry. I didn't want to go to the cookhouse, it might be on fire. But we were hardly given time to queue up and eat anything before we had to be lined up outside again and marched back to the accommodation.

Back on our "block" the female soldier welcomed us briefly and explained she was our platoon sergeant. She was a Staff Sergeant and we were to call her "Staff".

She seemed absolutely terrifying.   She also explained that we would have a platoon commander, a female captain, who would address us the next morning. "Reveille" would be at 5.30, breakfast at 6.00. Meanwhile we were left to unpack. The first thing I had to check was that "Reveille", (confusingly pronounced revalley), meant getting-up-time. It was then obvious to all, from the very beginning, that I was very green. Tentatively we started to get to know each other. Apparently there were 2 platoons of women. We were "2 platoon, Edinburgh Company", with 24 members and "1 platoon" also had 24 members. Mostly the 2 platoons would be trained separately; it seemed we wouldn't see much of the men for now.

I kept gleaning information from the other girls who all seemed much younger than me. A couple were only 18 so I must have seemed ancient to them. I was rather conscious of that fact.   Not all had gone to Roedean, Cheltenham Girls College, Gourdonstone and Benenden although some had. Most seemed friendly and all a bit subdued.   The bare corridors echoed with our movements. Some tried to cheer the place up with a spot of music.   There was a single phone at the end of the corridor but there was about as much chance of getting on it as getting a decent bed; someone always seemed to be someone using it, drinking up drops of comfort from parents and distant boyfriends.   Mobile phones would have been an ultimate luxury. We hadn't even heard of such an invention.

I set my alarm, appalled at the idea of getting up at 5.30. As I tried to get to sleep I thought back to my little office in Leicester Square. Already it seemed on another planet, up there in the night sky. So did my parents and everything hitherto familiar. Oh God, had I done the right thing?

Chapter 7 – So This Is It

I woke up, in the middle of the night, with a terrible start. It was pitch black, cold. There seemed to be some kind of emergency. Someone was shouting their head off up the corridor. I shot out of bed and out into the corridor, heart pounding, rushing to see who was in difficulty, my brain only just managing to grasp where I was. The corridor was a jumble of girls looking sleepy and scared. Was there a fire? No. We'd all been shocked out of our beds by Staff shouting this "Revalley" we'd been promised. All around alarm clocks buzzed unnecessarily. Staff ignored them, and barked at us to be dressed, and lined up outside in 15 minutes, ready to be marched to the cookhouse. We scattered, feeling drained, weak. She wandering around barking at anything she didn't like the look of, which seemed to be everything. My heart still thumping from the whole experience, I didn't really have time to consider what a novel way of waking up this had been, and whether it had met with any of my vague expectations of life at Sandhurst.

Outside it was freezing, dark and misty. It all felt surreal as we were marched down to the cookhouse. I say "marched," quite frankly I couldn't even feel my feet, let alone coordinate them. Once there I'd have eaten anything I was so hungry. But yet again we hardly had time to queue and eat before we had to be outside again ten minutes later.

We were barked back to the block and stood to attention whilst more things were explained. We were to get our uniforms from the Quartermaster's stores and the tailors were coming to measure us for our formal uniforms – Number Twos, and Mess Dress. Number Twos? Mess Dress? In the afternoon we were to be given a Basic Fitness Test, and meet our platoon commander. Staff also said she would put our programme for the next few weeks on the wall for us to study. We would get our own copies in due course. Now that would be interesting.

My confidence, already draining away fast as everything came to me as a complete surprise, was not helped by my thoughts about the ankle. Would it stand up to a Basic Fitness Test? What was a Basic Fitness Test? I sought out the attractive girl in the room next to mine. Her name was Tina. She was one of the very young ones – eighteen - but mature, I thought, sensible and friendly. She explained that the test was a timed run. She was nervous too.

"Shall we run together?" She suggested. "Encourage each other?"

I nearly snapped her hand off I was so grateful. And despite the age difference we became the firmest of friends from that moment. Odd how the oldest and the youngest were attracted to each other.

Off we were marched to get our uniforms. The female corporal at the Quartermaster's stores had obviously been doling out kit to green females like me countless times. And was fed up with it. Fed up with ignorant wannabes.

Her eyes very sharp she snapped at me, "and what size are you?" My reply, "..urm, I'm not too sure in those, may I try them on?" was not greeted cordially. Instead, she eyed me up and down frostily, and started piling items onto the bench between us.

"These should do." The pile grew alarmingly as I stood staring vacantly. Jackets, trousers, socks, T-shirts, jumpers, an assortment of hats. "My God," I thought, "is she going to give me regulation pyjamas and knickers?" I didn't dare ask.

"Try those against you," she snapped again holding out combat trousers. They were an explosion of green and brown colours. To me they looked the real thing. I started to feel quite excited, and held them up against me proudly.

"Dreadful," came the snap as she grabbed them off me, "try these." Eventually, and grovelling my thanks now, I had all the kit. Even those combat boots that had given my poor mother such horrors. The corporal turned her frost onto the next candidate. I escaped into the winter sunshine, and off to be measured for the more formal kit.

The tailors, being smart London civilian outfitters, were all politeness. Nothing was too much trouble which seemed odd after the corporal. I saw what the mess dress was like for the first time and thought it was very special. All cream and gold brocade, with a long green, silk sash over one shoulder. A Norman Hartnell number no less. Of course at this stage I hadn't seen myself actually wearing one. That disappointment came later.   The tube-like design of the dress didn't flatter the woman with any stomach.   The Number Twos, (dress uniform), looked terribly smart.   The room in Old College where we were measured for our fittings was absolutely lovely.   Grand, filled with light and oil paintings.   The beautiful view over the lawns went down to the large lake.   Once again I felt excited just to be where I was.   The Royal Military Academy, Sandhurst. The place itself was stunning.   I felt enormously privileged. Lucky by half.

The fittings over, it was back to lining up, more barking, and a desperate attempt to satisfy hunger in only a few moments at the cookhouse.   Warnings from other girls about not eating too much as we had to run soon afterwards were unnecessary.   The opportunity to have enough to eat, let alone too much, would have been most welcome.   But thoughts of, "Will the ankle stand up to this?" were overriding any thoughts of hunger, on this occasion anyway.   We lined up again, and marched to the barking.

Back at the block I used a whole can of Deep Heat on the ankle, and hid a "tubigrip" underneath my sock.   I donned the khaki kit and the boots for the first time.   We were to run in the boots.   They felt terribly heavy and awkward, enormous like twin aircraft carriers lashed up the ankles.   We'd only been given a few minutes to change, and my fingers trembled with haste and nerves. I could hear other girls chatting, and clumping down the corridor – how had they managed to change so quickly? My hair wouldn't stay up.   I fumbled with grips.   They had a life of their own as they kept dropping, seemingly magnetised to the floor. Out of time I flew down the corridor, out of the door, and into line.

We marched off to the start line where the rules were explained. PT staff were holding stop watches. The by now all too familiar sickness in my stomach. Now I would find out whether I could stand the pace and run quickly enough. Tina smiled at me. I smiled back. Then the roar: "Go," and we were off. PT staff screaming at us to run faster. Tina and I stayed close. We found ourselves saying, "Come on, you can do it," to each other. Heart pounding. Ankle OK. Towards the end we encouraged each other to put on a bit of a spurt. I wasn't at all sure where mine came from, but I wasn't going to let Tina spurt without me, I was going to stick to her like glue. We reached the end, and someone actually said "Well Done." I was thrilled, so was Tina. We'd apparently passed, actually two of the quickest, and I'd made a friend for life. Tina and I made a pact to always run together.

We weren't given time to dwell on our success, or otherwise. Immediately we were lined up, barked at, and marched to our classroom where we met our platoon commander. Captain Sanders.

"Good afternoon ladies," her mouth beamed at us. I'd never seen anything like it. At first, all I saw was her mouth, or rather her mouth full of large teeth, and her tongue relishing long slides around them. As if she was relishing licking us into shape. "My name is Captain Sanders. I am your platoon commander. Welcome to Sandhurst. So hands up those who failed their BFT please." One or two raised their hands weakly. "You are going to try harder aren't you?" continued the good captain. "You will put in some extra runs in the mornings won't you?" An order. "The next BFT will take place on Friday. All will pass please." The "please" didn't sound like a request.

Captain Sanders then gave us quite a talk about what a privilege it was to be there, how not all of us would see it through to the end but she hoped most of us would. We would learn what it was like to be really cold, really exhausted, really hungry, really wet, and really afraid.

"Does sound a real privilege," I couldn't help musing.

She hoped that we would all learn mutual respect for one another, and that we would all be able to help each other out during the next months. Then followed our first lesson in military law.

So the next few days went on. The programme kept us busy from 5.30 in the morning until well after midnight. Every morning we were inspected at muster parade, and any speck of dust, or crease in the wrong place was pounced upon with severity. As I was about the world's worst ironer this kept me very busy. I could spend 2 hours ironing a crease into a pair of trousers,. inspecting it, cursing, trying again. Going cross-eyed into the early hours. Those who had some military background – either family, or Officer Cadet Training Corps, or the Territorial Army – certainly had an edge. Bulling boots came as a bit of a shock, I'd never heard of spitting on my shoes to make them shine. How did one produce the best spit for polishing?

The worst mornings were when the rooms were inspected too. Usually by the terrifying Staff but sometimes by the awesome Captain too. Exhausted in the early hours, I'd still be smearing "Brasso" all over the shop. Eyes bleary. Trying to bring a shine to radiator stops, hidden coat pegs, and window latches lurking behind curtains. They looked everywhere, desperate to find a smear, a speck or a lack of sparkle. And they could really shout at you, make you feel as small as the speck they'd just found.

I tried not to look at the programme for the following weeks too often. It induced a painful lack of sleep. If I knew what I had to endure too long before I had to endure it, I'd lie awake all night, desperately tired, but desperately worried. I dreaded the long runs. It was so cold that January that the lungs began to hurt after the first few miles.

However, what I dreaded most was the first exercise we had to go on. I'd no idea what to expect and, if I'd had an idea (even a small one), I'd have dreaded it much more. I worked on the premise that the less I knew the less sleep I'd lose. It didn't always work for the best. Sometimes the shock of what we had to do nearly knocked me out of my boots. We'd only been there a few days when we were marched to a large, fast-flowing stream in full combat kit, complete with backpack. We were ordered into the stream. It was icy cold.

We were told to look upstream. There the water disappeared into a long, black, narrow pipe. We were ordered to go, one by one, into the icy water through the blackness of the unlit pipe until we eventually found the other end and popped out. The only way to go with the stream through the pipe was to slither like a snake aiming, with stout determination, to keep the face above the freezing water. Had I really volunteered for this?

No. Well, not in my right mind. No-one said much. One girl wailed, "Oh f...," and another "you must be joking." But we all knew it wasn't much of a joke, and when the order came to "Disappear Now" the first girl jumped in and started wading towards the pipe. Then the next, and the next. When it came to my turn I decided just to do it as quickly as I could without thinking. The cold numbed my brain a bit, but I knew that if I hesitated for a moment and started to think about it, I would be there for hours hesitating, prevaricating, pleading, afraid and humiliated. It went that way for one or two of the others

As if that wasn't quite enough for one day we were marched onto the Assault Course. Yet another horrible shock to me. Huge pieces of kit. High. As high as very tall houses, even blocks of flats. We were asked who was afraid of heights and one or two admitted it. That was the first time I'd seen knees literally knock together. This was also the first time that I'd ever considered climbing something so ridiculous but, mercifully, I'd never been afraid of heights. Climbing the stairs at home had never presented any problem. And I'd always been able to look out of my bedroom window without feeling dizzy. We were told to start climbing one of the instruments of torture. And so I began. Up and up I went. And then I looked down. The ground began to swirl below my eyes. I looked up again quickly.

"I am afraid of heights," I blurted out too late, "This sort of height anyway." There was nothing to break a fall should we slip.

My hands sweated and my grip felt weak. I started to shake. Those that had admitted to a fear were given extra help and encouragement; I was shouted at to continue. Slowly up I went, too terrified to look down but ever conscious of that swirling ground hard beneath me. I got to a small platform. A few others were already there and in turn we were told to grab hold of a pulley. It was attached to a long rope. Over a large lake. It was bitterly cold and the sweat on my body and clothes was beginning to freeze onto me. I grabbed the pulley when it was my turn. Then steeled myself to jump into the air, gripping the bar of the pulley as it plunged down the rope and over the lake. The cold air rushed into my lungs. "Oooooooh", I wailed as the pulley rushed me down. Of course, as a nice little touch at the bottom, the rope ended just short and we all got another soaking. What a day. Definitely quite a punishing sort of day.

There was one big plus on this course. The other girls were great, and after only a few days I had my favourites. Tina of course, then there was Jemima, tall, blonde, elegant down to her toe nails and stunningly beautiful. We could time how long it took for all eyes to turn to her when she entered a room: about 3 seconds. She was also totally irreverent, laughed a dirty laugh like a disgusting blocked drain. I adored and envied her chutzpah. Then there was mad Gloria, where had they found her?

"Oh Gilli," she would say, "you're a marvel." She'd then giggle and wriggle alarmingly, "Do show me how you managed to tie your boot laces so beautifully." She really was incapable; incapable of running, incapable of doing up her buttons on her shirt. There was always one button too many at the collar if she wasn't assisted.

Somehow I was drawn to Gloria. Fascinated by her ineptitude and delighted to have found someone more useless than me. Then there was Joan, very young and desperate to remain cheerful, even when tears were flowing down her pretty face. (Beautiful mop of short black curls.) And there was Tamsin; over-competent in everything except her tolerance of people. We were a real mixed bunch thrown in together, stirred and cooking together. Not one of them fitted in with my stereotyped image of a typical female army officer. Here was an intelligent, feminine, bright and warm group of women. Our search for a challenge, an adventure, drew us together to this place. And yes, there was the stirring of a desire to serve our Queen and country. To do something noble, useful, important, be part of something with such a deep sense of tradition, history, honour, valour. Maybe some tiny bit of it could rub off on us. Difficult to explain or describe. Perhaps to put something back. It was no coincidence then that up there on the wall of Old College was the Sandhurst motto: "To serve to lead."

That first week though we all suffered from the same shock and confusion as to why, of all places on God's earth, we had wanted to be here. (And quite a lot of homesickness hung around too.) Civilian life had receded so far out of my consciousness that I simply couldn't imagine what it was like to live life without that tinge of dread as to what was going to happen next.

Chapter 8 – Left Out In The Cold

What did happen next was that we were sent on our first Exercise. We had to absolutely stuff our rucksacks full of kit in such a way that we could pull out any item at the drop of a hat when ordered to. If any of the directing staff should say:

"Produce your left bootlace," at any time during the day or night, we had to be able to instantly locate it. All our kit would be inspected at nice little surprise inspections throughout the exercise. Night or day. Not at all like a party game. Since I didn't really have any clear idea at all as to what an "Exercise" might consist of I had a kind of dull sickness and dread in my stomach. I'd been told I would now learn what it felt like to be cold, tired and hungry. It was fortunate I didn't know more and, not having had the luxury of seeing or hearing any news since we'd been at Sandhurst, none of us knew that this was the coldest January ever on record. We had grasped, however, that it was bitterly cold, and we were all in a panic trying to get extra kit. Some of the girls knew one or two of the men, (I'd hardly even managed to spot one thus far but hadn't really tried – I'd accepted that I'd had my chance and was over the hill), and they'd apparently charmed some extra kit from them. Tina had done well! So had the gorgeous Jemima! These were the girls I decided to befriend.

We were allowed to go to bed early the night before. I probably got into mine around 11 exhausted as usual having packed my kit, unpacked it all, fiddled with it, and repacked it until I felt I was going mad. "Revalley" was at 1 am. Was it worth going to bed at all? I stumbled into the sheets, and as my head touched the pillow was startled to hear the alarm going off. I rose reluctant and groggy and started checking my kit again. We were, as ever, marched to the cookhouse for breakfast. The frost glistened in the light from the windows.

"Who could possibly eat at this hour, in these circumstances?" I moaned, as Tamsin sensibly stuffed her face. Gloria was whinging about her bootlaces again, and Jemima was laughing at how awful we looked. I certainly felt awful but had long since stopped considering, let alone worrying about, what I looked like. We were marched back to the block to collect our kit and lined up outside before being unceremoniously shoved into the backs of 4-tonne trucks, and driven away to some secret destination. In the pitch black night air, I listened to the distinctive rumble of the vehicle and, looking out into the twinkling sky I wondered what my friends would say if they could see me now.

"Well, we all wondered why the hell you were so keen, Gilli.... We did try to tell you.... to warn you........." I couldn't even pretend this was glamorous, or fun. This really was it. We had begun to train in earnest. Exercises mimic real war conditions. When all was said and done, whatever my motives, I was being trained to fight, to survive in war. I felt lonely, afraid, unprepared and utterly incompetent.

We were emptied from the lorry in what looked like a forest clearing. We were given black paint to smear on our faces, and told to collect ferns and twigs to decorate our combat helmets. This injected a bit of humour as we all tried to squint from behind bits of twigs. We were beginning to look unrecognisable, indistinct from the trees around us.

Someone began to shout: "Line up. Now." And, "Quick march." I started, hoping it would warm me up a bit. The pack on my back seemed terribly heavy, and the boots not terribly comfortable. Marching felt like the last thing I could do. Then, "Run!" came the order.

"Oh surely not," I thought, "surely, surely not." But we did start to run, me in a bit of a panic as to why it should be necessary. Everything was still taking me by surprise. I was still trying to apply logic when I didn't understand the "Whys and Wherefores".

At last, totally done in, we were ordered to stop. We were in another clearing, and this time several Directing Staff were present. There were Land Rovers, a tent and wonderful smells. Another breakfast, out came the mess tins and in went everything on offer. I was starving and it was still only 7.30 am. Steaming hot tea from my big plastic bucket of a mess cup. I could have lain down, right there and then, and slept for a fortnight. I could have………

However, that was not the plan. We were in groups of six, taking it in turns to be in command and then the radio operator. The radio was an enormous, heavy piece of kit. The first in command was sent to receive orders from a male captain while all the Directing Staff watched and took note of every move we made, and every sound we uttered: every moan, every whinge, every curse or "Ooops. Sorry." By the time our leader came back the cold was beginning to feel unbearable. The male captain came over and helpfully told us that, so long as we kept our "core" warm, we'd be OK. It didn't matter if the rest of our body was freezing we'd apparently happily survive, as long as the core stayed warm. I found this not a jot comforting. I didn't wish to "survive", I wanted to be warm. All over. Anyway what was this core? I wasn't an apple. According to the good Captain "Any fool could be cold." Well, I was certainly cold and I did feel rather a fool for being in the middle of a freezing forest in the middle of winter in the middle of the night. The Captain continued to drone on. We must apparently get plenty of hot food and drink hot drinks, wear as much kit as we could fit on. That was our responsibility, apparently. "Thanks a bunch" was written all over our faces.

I've never been able to forget that little pep talk, no matter how hard I try I always think of my core when I'm cold. I wonder if that Captain has forgotten it?

Then the exercise began in earnest. We were given a grid reference to locate on our maps and our goal was to reach it, preferably before nightfall. There were little obstacles on the way: like large rivers to cross, ravines to traverse, cliffs to climb and bogs in unhelpful places. Apparently we might also bump into "the enemy". Blimey all in a day's work. Off we went, the directing Staff, (we called them The DS), watched at a distance. It was very hard going, hard underfoot, the kit becoming heavier and heavier. We tried not to squabble over short-cuts. We tried not to squabble over when it was time to have a sit down. Lunch, from our rations, was delicious we were so hungry. But always we were trying to hurry so as not to lose points by being late. It took all day to reach our destination. We were exhausted but relieved to arrive. In another clearing in another forest........or the same one? We'd no idea. We just hoped we'd "passed". Once we met up with the other teams we immediately started to swap horror stories. Then we were told to put up our 2-woman tents in a defensive position, (apparently in case of attack during the night), and to go to the cook-tent for food. Everything and anything edible on offer disappeared within minutes. Then we started on our emergency rations of Mars Bars and other chocolates.   Nothing seemed to satisfy the need for calories.

By 10 pm it was so cold that we couldn't stop our bodies from shaking.   It was pitch dark again and I was in a tent with a good friend, Monica. She'd been one of the marvels who'd managed to borrow some extra kit from a boy on the course.   As it wasn't our turn to keep watch we decided to settle down and rest.   Monica kindly said I could share the borrowed bivi bag, (a special sleeping bag that went over the normal sleeping bag for extra warmth).   I was terribly grateful.   Neither of us could bear to take any clothes off, not even our boots.   So we struggled, giggling, into our separate sleeping bags and then tried to get both of us into the one bivi bag.   The absurdity of the whole situation in the middle of this frozen forest struck us both as hilarious, and several times we were told to "Keep it down".

Eventually we agreed we'd have to take off the boots.   We unglued ourselves from each other and wrestled with freezing fingers to get the boots off.   Then we started the whole process again, more hilarious giggles, and more angry shouts from the DS which reduced us to helpless idiots "shushing" each other like two drunken teenagers.   At last we, and our sleeping bags, were in.   You couldn't have got a Mars bar wrapper between us, it was that tight.   But we did keep each other warm.

The DS were apparently slightly concerned about the extreme temperature, and sent off a couple of corporals in a Land Rover to buy up the whole stock of chocolate in a local shop, wherever that was.   It couldn't have been very local.   We were so isolated.   But we certainly needed the energy, I'd never eaten so much in my life, let alone so much chocolate.   It had to be eaten quickly or it just froze solid.

When it came to my turn to keep watch I was so reluctant to get out and do my stint that I couldn't have cared less who or what wanted to attack us.

"Just let them," I thought. "So what? I'd rather be shot at than have to get out of this bag." However, I knew that wasn't playing the game, so Monica and I had to wriggle and jiggle again, this time bad-tempered, tetchy and dying to simply go back to sleep. I had to keep watch for an hour, the longest hour ever. I had to lie on my belly in the snow, pretending to keep my sub-machine gun (unloaded) ready to fire in the right direction. Who cared what the right direction was? My teeth chattered uncontrollably. It was 2.30 in the morning, what the hell was I doing? Such thoughts didn't really help.

My watch over, I didn't feel I should wake Monica by attempting the almost impossible and squeezing into the bag yet again. But I did.

"Sorry Monica," I lied, whispering.

"Uh" came the reply as we wriggled and jiggled. This time it was not funny.

We were woken at 5. Everyone had suffered terribly with the cold. I was all for canonising Monica for having known a boy who had a bivi bag. Breakfast was the most welcome ever, the hot tea the greatest gift God ever gave. We went through the same process as the day before. But a different leader. Me the radio operator. My ankle was aching horribly, the radio was heavy and I must admit I said the most banal things into it. No-one had ever taught me radio language but I knew I was being listened to and judged so I thought I might earn points if I pretended to be coping admirably with the hardships and appeared good-natured about the whole ghastly thing. So I breezed "Hullo" cheerily every time someone tried to contact us.

"It's number 3 group here, we're all fine. Enjoying the fresh air. Lovely countryside." Eventually the DS could stand it no longer.

"Miss Wright, for God's sake stop chatting into the radio as though you were on a vicar's picnic," somebody at the other end snapped. "Restrict yourself to facts, and get someone to teach you how to speak on the radio. NOW." No points there I feared.

After lunch we were given a command task to do. I'd had enough of these things when I was trying to get into Sandhurst. Now I was into Sandhurst, I was a bit put out that they'd cropped up again. This command task seemed to involve a lot of water, in the form of a river, and logs and I had this blessed radio too. I can't say it was fun. I can't say I did any better than I'd ever done before. In fact I think my group did very badly. No points there either. It wasn't going well.

I wasn't sure I could handle another night. We all felt the same but didn't want anyone to think we were weakening, so we all kept up the pretence. Monica exceeded canonisation by agreeing to share the boy's bag again. I thought this was heroic. We didn't giggle at all though, just wrestled in silence. The DS had more chocolate rations which again were consumed in record time. We couldn't clean our teeth, the toothpaste was frozen solid. We must have looked and smelt pretty rough. I was struggling to continue wearing contact lenses but, as my solution was also frozen, I just kept them in all night.

Worse was to come. Next morning, after little sleep, I was called to be the one in charge, solely responsible for leading my group to their next destination. Me. On my own. Being watched. Judged. I'd never read a map before and only just learnt about grid references in the classroom last week. I'd never used a compass until last week on Barossa – a wilder part of Sandhurst's grounds. I'd never tried to lead a group anywhere, never mind across rough terrain to somewhere I didn't know.

"Just be cheerful, and pretend to be enthusiastic," I told myself. "Don't let them see the terror in your eyes." Yet again, I remembered that I was the oldest and piled extra pressure on myself...... the oldest I must also be the best. I listened hard to the male captain's orders that I was to relay to my group. I scribbled with cold fingers anything I thought might be relevant while watching my icy breath making steam trains. "This is it," I thought, all negative thoughts flooding in. "This is where I show myself for what I am, not really Sandhurst stuff." I trundled back to my expectant group, and did my best to give them orders. I tried to sound confident as I stumbled over the detail, unsure of the all-important grid reference now. I chivvied them to collect their stuff and prepare for our "H hour", time to be off.

We studied the map, studied our compasses, and set off. After a while I was surprised to see the sun breaking through the cloud, as if saying a cheery "Hi, get on with it then, it's not so bad you know", and it did cheer me up no end. How dependent we were on the elements. I'd never been so close to nature before. The sun shining, even for a few minutes, was like a reminder of an old friend, warm and cheerful.

We trudged on. There were the usual, quite understandable complaints from the radio operator as she stumbled with the unkind kit. I was concerned with keeping everyone moving as Staff and Captain Sanders were never far behind, always watching. We lunched

59

from our rations as usual. Most of us, having already eaten our chocolate for the whole exercise, were jealously trying to wheedle some from the thrifty ones who'd sensibly saved some of theirs. We were terribly careful not to let the DS see us being anything but coping and in control. All rather forced. Actually this was getting more and more difficult as bad tempers were erupting all over the shop at this stage. Things were getting harder to bear. How come Staff and Captain Sanders were looking so clean and bright? Where were they sleeping? We wondered.

After lunch we trudged again. I was concerned that our surroundings didn't seem to match what I thought the map was telling us. However, we'd been told countless times to "trust the compass" and it seemed to be pointing us onwards. So I led them onwards. Straight up to a very large river.

"What the hell is that doing there?" I panicked taking a frenzied look at the map. No river there. No-one looked very pleased. I strained my eyes looking for non-existent bridges. I struggled to think how we could get across - improbable.

Staff and Captain Sanders watched with interest, keen to see what I'd do next. I wished I knew. I sat down in the grass, we all sat down.

"I've blown it haven't I?" I looked at Captain Sanders, a lead brick in the pit of my stomach. She came over to me.

"Well, Miss Wright," she asked, "what have we got here?"

"A river ma'am," I replied, stating the obvious. "I don't really think it's supposed to be here. It's not on the map you see," I finished weakly, hoping she'd agree or give me a clue - a tiny nugget of comfort. Nothing was forthcoming. I tried again.

"I think we're supposed to get somewhere over there." I wafted my arm about uncertainly in a broad, sweeping semi-circle. My lower lip began to tremble.

"But I don't know how to get there now. I don't know where I've gone wrong I'm afraid."

"Well don't start to lose it," she said firmly. "Study the map again Miss Wright. Then check your compass. Take some suggestions from the team. Hear what they have to say. Think about it Miss Wright."

She walked away. I was not discouraged, on the contrary. It didn't sound as if we'd got to go all the way back and start again. I would have been lynched by my team deservedly if we had. We'd all had enough. After some discussion and more study of map and compass we amended my plan and set off again. This time Staff and Captain Sanders walked with us rather than a little distance behind. Captain Sanders was actually chatting, asking me questions about my previous life. I was really grateful to her. It made me feel better to think I was worth talking to after my useless efforts to lead the team up a gumtree. We'd only a couple more miles to go, it seemed, and the atmosphere was lighter now, we were almost jolly, perhaps we were so tired we'd entered another level of existence, but with a tinge of hope. We didn't think we'd beat the other teams but that no longer mattered. We were going to get there. Relief bred cheerfulness.

We arrived at the next camp just after darkness fell. Again it was bitterly cold. But the cookhouse tent glowed brightly. The smells were intoxicating and there were fresh chocolate rations. We scoffed - no other word for it – and we prepared our base for our last night out. (For this time anyway.) Monica looked resigned

61

at my pleading smile. The bivi bag, I'm sure it saved my life. There was more awful guard duty in the middle of the freezing night. The stars glowing like twinkling icicles in the black sky seen through a clearing in the forest. My hands ached dreadfully with the cold, but I wasn't the only one. We all felt it.

Next morning we all felt better, pretty sure we could survive now. We'd be back in that luxury item – the iron single bed – by evening. There was no let-up though. At 7.30 am we were attacked. It still wasn't light, and the loud explosions seemingly inside the tents, and the screaming came as a huge surprise. We hadn't really taken "being attacked" seriously at all and, as we fumbled in the cold, the shock of it galvanised us, all shouting at once. I felt the panic and chaos. As we had to sleep with our weapons they weren't hard to find. It was those poor sods who'd taken their boots off that I felt sorry for: their hands frozen, the darkness and all those lace holes, and live laces wriggling around like little snakes.

"Oh help," wailed Gloria, ever true to form. "Help, please, my laces, my boots." She continued ad infinitum.

"Oh somebody help her for God's sake," we all snapped, nobody rushing at once.

The attack was pretty short-lived. A bit half-hearted after the initial enthusiasm, thank God. I don't think I ever saw any enemy. They could probably smell the cookhouse tent as well as we could. We just heard the bangs, the screams, smelt the smoke and nearly choked on it. Then thankfully it all faded away fairly quickly.

"I guess we do look a scary bunch," I laughed because I knew it was, at last, time for breakfast. And, as always, I was starving.

Then came a long march, with full kit of course. A command task – not so much of a shock now, but still I felt a tinge of dread at having to face another one. Some lunch, and then, to my utter disbelief, a race. A race after all that! However, when the time came, to my complete amazement I was one of the quickest. Admittedly everyone was exhausted, but I was delighted, and ended the whole rotten episode on a real high. Then at last into a 4-tonne truck back to Sandhurst, which now felt like Home. And I longed to be there.

Chapter 9 – Light at The End of the Tunnel

There was no day off, let alone a week-end, to recover from the traumas of our first exercise as officer cadets. The next day was a normal Sandhurst day, "Revalley" long before the "sparrows". But something was different, I"d lost at least a stone in weight over those last few days. Nothing fitted and I'd never been so slim despite having stuffed and stuffed chocolate by the shed load. I was quite pleased with my new body. No, I was actually delighted! It felt great! I knew it was the person inside that mattered most. After all I'd drummed this common sense into my consciousness for years. I'd always felt that other girls were the slim ones, the attractive ones. So, somehow, it helped my confidence to be slimmer now myself. Odd or not, I did feel more acceptable, and somehow that mattered to me.

Also I was fit. This felt absolutely wonderful, to be able to run, distances, through woods, across fields, to spur the body on, to feel that energy and control. It was a wonderful feeling of independence and power. If nothing else I was truly glad that I'd experienced this feeling before I died.

The cold must have helped us to burn up the calories and the spare body fat. It had been So Cold. Do you know what we found out once we were safely back at Sandhurst? Something very interesting, and very galling. The men had also gone out on exercise on exactly the same night as us, to a nearby location. Their first night out, they'd been preparing their base when they received a call from their Headquarters and they were summoned back to Sandhurst. And why? Apparently because it was too cold for them to stay out.

We, being some of the first women to ever go to Sandhurst for Officer Training, must have had something to prove, so the female big-wigs left us out to get on with it. Well, we certainly did prove something. We proved we could get the first stages of frost-bite, to say nothing of the most outrageous blisters. Several of our number had to go to the Medical Centre for treatment for shin splints, torn muscles and ligaments, frost-nip and so on. Some simply didn't come back on the course. They couldn't face any more and who could blame them? I was astonished that none of us got pneumonia, but I'm not even sure we got colds.

My parents were pleased to hear from me. When I eventually got through. It seemed my mother had had less sleep than me recently, worried sick about me out in that cold.

But at least we had the first exercise out of the way, only several more to come. It was understandable that, at this stage, some decided not to continue. They just realised that Sandhurst, and the Army, was not for them after all. I felt that it was very brave of them, to be honest like that.

I realised I'd learnt an awful lot in the last couple of weeks. But only enough to make me see how much more there was to learn. There was still an awesome way to go and I still didn't want to look further than the next day, I just couldn't deal with the anticipation. For me there was something to dread every day: inspections of rooms, of kit, of person; long marches with kit; runs with or without kit. I think I even managed to dread the swimming sessions. And there were endless Command tasks with heavy logs and much water. We seemed to be on the go twenty-four hours a day, and seven days a week. What I vowed I would never forget is how much you can get done in five minutes, if focussed - by a ferocious staff sergeant. There was always so much to do, and everything we did we had to be in the correct dress, which was always different from the one we seemed to be wearing. We'd be marched back to the block and, if lucky, given four minutes to change, be immaculate and back outside, lined up ready for inspection. Washing and ironing our own clothes was of course a prerequisite. I spent ages ironing late at night, trying to get the right crease in the right place, until I went cross-eyed. I was finding life gruelling, punishing physically and emotionally and psychologically. And the punishment was my payment in a way. And it was my new life.

Every so often we were marched across the grounds to a huge hall we called the Sleeping Bag. We dreaded this place. It was warm. There were no windows and the sound of the lighting hummed like a distant droning bee. No fresh air. Some big-wig would lecture us (with the men – at last I spotted some), on some terribly important aspect of war, the history of war, the strategy of war, leadership, and so on. It always seemed to be after lunch, and we were always short of sleep. Trying to keep eyes open was like long, slow torture, they were so desperate to close, to slip into that appealing state of sleep. I will never know how my eyes managed to stay open, I feared the reprisals I suppose. There were a few hundred of us in that hall, but if one eye closed the culprit was spotted instantly. And jumped on by what seemed to be a herd of tanks. All weapons firing at once. At close range. Straight at them. The culprit was humiliated. Punished. Marched out. Screamed at. Of course we all tried to help each other to stay awake. Prodding and poking and shaking as surreptitiously as possible. But it was almost impossible some days. There was always someone nodding off.

One thing about these early weeks which was so rewarding was the friendships. We all got to know each other pretty quickly and pretty well. And mostly I liked all the girls. Very much indeed. When one was down and having a good sob the rest would rally round and cheer her up. There was always something to laugh at with Jemima around. We did get thoroughly fed up. We did get tired, cold, hungry. We did all have to face challenges that mirrored our worst nightmares. But somehow the camaraderie, the laughs we had, the tight, fiercely loyal friendships made it much more bearable. We laughed at things we could never have found funny in civilian life.

And talking of civilian life. It had completely disappeared from the face of the earth. One day a civilian car was parked on the parade ground. One of the girls spotted it from a window and shouted out.

"A civilian car. On the parade ground. Look. Really. It's RED!" We all rushed to have a look.

"Gosh, so it is. Doesn't it look strange. Seems so peculiar to see a real civilian car. And bright red. How odd that looks". Civvy street and all its many colours seemed to have been wiped from our memories.

The programme ground on relentlessly. Every day a long, full and exhausting day. And then, at last, it seemed we had arrived at the end of the programme for the first 5 weeks. This was quite a watershed. We all had to be interviewed individually by the DS. To discuss our performance and progress, or lack of it. And some of our number would be leaving. Either for good, "because it had become clear that their talents were better suited to civilian life", or to start again with the new intake next term. "Back-termed" it was called. To my complete relief, I'd survived. Not with any brilliance, but it seemed I was getting a bit more competent. And then we were given our first week-end off. We could even go home. A friend of mine very kindly came to fetch me, and I sat back whilst I was driven to my parents' house 3 hours away. Not having to do anything for the first time ever – or so it seemed.

Chapter 10 – Going up in smoke

I got to my parents' house late that Friday evening. It all felt like something from a previous life. Misty memories of being safe, cosy, warm. They were overjoyed to see me and marvelled at my new figure. They also wanted to know all the news. I could only beg to be allowed to go to bed. Apparently all my friends and relations wanted to see me, to ask me how it was going, what I'd had to suffer. So, had I been forgiven? Had I managed to purge away the guilt of a cancelled wedding with all that physical and mental punishment I'd suffered at Sandhurst? In truth all I wanted to do was sleep that week-end. It was wonderful to have no programme and not to be rushed every minute of the day from 5.30 am onwards, not to have to continually change outfit. So it was a bit of a juggle really, a compromise between what was wanted from me and what I wanted. I don't think anyone could have had a clue just how much sleep I needed to catch up on, no matter how willing they were. Nor could they understand just how strange everything felt. No Staff shouting orders at me, having to take the initiative myself. I felt a bit lost really.

All too soon it was over, Sunday afternoon arrived, and the same friend was over-generous and drove me back down to Sandhurst. Back in the block we all chatted away ten to the dozen. We'd all had a great week-end. We'd all wanted to luxuriate the hours away in bed. We were happily exchanging news in the block when Staff came in.

"In Lines. In the Corridor. Don't just Stand There. Now!"

And back we went to normal. But from now on we did get time off at week-ends. Not whole week-ends of course. But after lessons on Saturday we usually got the afternoon off. And sometimes we got time off on Sundays too. It was all too much. So much time all to ourselves. However, the programme seemed just as difficult. Just as packed. Just as exhausting.

We went off on another exercise, and it was warmer this time, although it was still Winter. The end of this exercise involved teams building a raft, after searching for bits of wood, and having a raft race. We all sank.

68

There was a lot of shouting. Some laughter. A lot of wet people.

I still didn't like to look too far ahead in the programme. It continued to be the case that every day there was something to dread. In a Big Way. One day I saw "NBC Training" for the following afternoon. All afternoon.

"What's this NBC Training?" I asked Tina.

"Nuclear, Biological and Chemical warfare training," came the reply.

"Good God. What the hell are they going to expect us to do?" I was alarmed. Who wouldn't be? Tina didn't really know much more which I think that was a good thing. I'm not sure I could have joined in that afternoon if I had known what it was all about. First we had to march to the Quartermasters stores to be given our gas masks. Then we marched to a far corner of the Sandhurst grounds.

To start, Staff and Captain Sanders explained quite a bit about chemical warfare. It was very interesting. Very depressing.

"How could human beings do that to other human beings?" I kept thinking. Then we were told all about "Naps" tablets that we could take if we ever found ourselves subjected to it. They were supposed to reverse some of the negative effects of contamination. None of us were convinced about that. We were also given pretend plastic needles to inject our thighs with another so-called antidote. None of us were convinced about that either. I could only believe that to be involved in either nuclear, biological or chemical warfare would be the End. To actually be on the battlefield with dead colleagues all around. There was no way I'd have the heart to inject myself with one of these plastic things. It

69

really would have to be the end for me. My thoughts on this horrific subject were utterly negative.

"Women on the front line?" I muttered. "I don't want any part in this. It's as evil and as cruel as anything I can imagine." But I didn't want the men involved either. No-one should be subjected to this. I couldn't help wondering how I'd feel in a real frontline situation when chemicals were being used. I realised I would fight with all my strength to preserve the lives of my colleagues, my friends and certainly my family. So just what could I become? What hidden capabilities were being stirred up in me? We were all looking dejected. Depressed. Apart from Tamsin who was always gung ho, always looking for points. Then the gas masks were explained. Horrid, black rubber things. And the oxygen canisters. We studied them. Had a try with them. We also played with Fullers Earth – another useful ingredient apparently in this context. Then we all had to squeeze into some bare little wooden hut. There were about 20 of us left on the course by now, huddled together in our NBC suits, holding onto our gas masks. The door was closed. Shut. But only after some foul smelling gas was thrown in with us. It went "pop", and,

"GAS GAS GAS" was screamed by the DS. Fumbling, and urgently we donned our masks. We heard nothing but our amplified breathing. We all looked dumbly through the masks. And we had to sit it out. Until we were given the all clear signal, and allowed to file out of the wooden door, take off the masks and breathe the air outside, deeply.

Then it was a nuclear explosion. A huge bang followed by much screaming and shouting. Donning of masks, and handfuls of fullers earth urgently applied, with anxious fingers. The naps tablets and the injections

70

administered by fumbling partners.　It was a surreal experience, at once both a nightmare scenario, and a meaningless game.　We were all affected by the potential horror.　For days we chatted amongst ourselves.　What would we really do in such a situation?　For real.　How would we really feel?　What would be our priorities? We'd been a bit cynical about the training.　Probably to protect us from our deeper feelings of horror which we simply couldn't face.　None of us had enjoyed it.　It had affected my consciousness and the horror of such evil stayed with me, and always will.

"Well, women want equality with the men," I thought.　"They want to be in combat.　To be treated in the same way.　But I don't.　I don't want any part of that. It is too unutterably horrific.　Even that half-day's training.　If that's equality.........."

To be frank this wasn't the first time I'd thought about this equality in the Armed Forces.　Once we actually started training with the men it was obvious that they were physically stronger.　But the women always had a great deal to offer.　In terms of planning, strategy, tactics, and we weren't always beaten by the men in the command tasks, or in the physical events.　The training didn't provide us with real situations, but they were sometimes incredibly realistic.　And what with the lack of sleep, the atmosphere created by all involved, well it did all feel real at times.　More than once I felt the sheer terror of war.　The horror of battle.　Of the weapons; injuries; naked fear of facing tortured undignified death; exhaustion, and panic.　And more than once out on exercise I thought, "I don't want equality thank you." And I meant it at the time.　I really did.

The realism of some of the exercises meant that we grew close to each other.　This dependence on each other for support bonded us very tightly. But at other times it was very much a lonely effort that was required. No-one could do the running for you. No-one else could summon up the inner reserves to survive the cold, the wet, the hunger and exhaustion. And so we were finding out about our own, hitherto, undiscovered strengths, or lack of them.

My very favourite part of the training at Sandhurst was the drill. The marching up and down and around that fabulous and historic parade square in those impressive and beautiful surroundings. I was useless at first. Couldn't work my right foot separately from my left. Couldn't swing my arms to the correct height. Didn't really know where they were ending up. I was told I was useless.

"Goose-stepping Miss Wright is not what we're here to do," screamed Staff and the drill sergeant together. For the first months I really struggled. But I wanted to do it. Like a child wanting to do something well. I felt the most fantastic tingle when we were all in step. Both women's platoons – about 30 of us by now in all. And when the band accompanied us, well, I went off into the stratosphere I was so delighted. Quite unlike anything I'd ever experienced. Real spine-tingling pleasure. True it was sadly so cold during that first term. Our combined breath formed a smoke-screen to hide our ineptitude. Except nothing could be hidden from these sergeant majors. They were so honed they sensed mistakes as well as heard and saw them.

One day we were practising drill. Terribly smart. Our matt leather shoes bulled until they looked like glass. Getting a bit more competent by this stage. We had been told that the Senior Division, (the intake before ours), would be "passing out" in April, and that we, the

Junior Division would take part in the passing out parade. This meant we had to have lots of extra practice. I was never completely relaxed about drill. I was never completely relaxed about anything at Sandhurst. But at least it meant I wasn't fearing for my life up cliffs, down caves, on the assault course, or on exercise. The concentration required for performing the marching and manoeuvres was intense, not a hair had to be out of place. If it was there was always Big Trouble. And no-one can shout insults like a sergeant major. Often they were extremely cutting but also extremely funny. They did have great senses of humour. But of course we couldn't laugh. Had to keep our faces straight. Had to keep perfectly still in fact, apart from the specific movements when ordered.

There was one day I recall so clearly. It was chilly to start with, but the sun came out later, and it was a really lovely bright day. We were rather startled when the Academy Sergeant Major Himself appeared on the parade square to take our drill practice. This had never happened before. A reverent ripple of:

"Oooh it's the Academy Sergeant Major," could be felt in the air, as our anxiety level rose. It was as if Yoda had appeared before us. The ASM was a Terribly Important Personage. He was revered by every single person at Sandhurst regardless of their rank. He was God around here. If we didn't do well then we'd be letting down Staff and Captain Sanders as well as each other, and there would be Trouble. This particular ASM had tremendous presence, he was the smartest person I'd ever come across. Everything that was meant to be shiny glowed. Everything that was meant to be pressed was crisp. His turn-out was immaculate. He stood 20 foot tall in our eyes. And could he shout? Could he scream? His orders were barked out like a new language. Very loud. We were doing our level best, but were a bit like a herd of nervous horses. It wasn't the most impressive performance and the ASM wasn't letting us get away with anything.

"What's wrong with your feet ma'am?" he bawled at close range to Gloria. Their noses almost touching. His eyebrows twitching with a life of their own.

"D-d-don't know.....s........" Gloria unfortunately responded.

"Shut up. Now. Don't ever answer back to meeeeeah, I don't want to converse with the likes of you. You're not at a tea party you're on My Parade Square. Ma'am." His voice screeched, storming off. Gloria's lower lip wobbled. She started to bite it. And then remembered not to.

We continued. It got quite warm. I began to feel hot inside my uniform. My forehead was perspiring. And then my nose started to itch. I tried to twitch it surreptitiously. A droplet was beginning to run down the inside of my nostrils. Tickling me as it moved along. Slowly. Irritating. It started to settle on the end of my nose. Maddening. I couldn't concentrate on anything else. Just this drop. We were standing to attention at the time, and I knew that the worst crime I could commit would be to move. Even slightly. But it really irritated. It really tickled. It was unbearable. I watched the ASM trying not to move my head, or even my eyes, and gradually, as the torture of this droplet built up to intolerable levels, I persuaded myself that I could move my hand so quickly across the end of my nose and bat it off before he saw anything. Big Mistake. Just as my arm began its sneaky ascent there was a thunderous bellow.

"Who is That Woman?" He roared in front of the whole of Sandhurst. Staff rushed to his side to give him my name. Although no-one dared move to look I still felt their full attention enthralled, transfixed. All focussed on me. Waiting for the next instalment. There was a horrible pause. Then a loud high-pitched scream.

"Get That Woman off My Parade Square. March her to the guardroom. Lock her up. Never let her see the light of day again. Let her know what it is to languish and consider her Horrible Crime. Ma'am." Soldiers instantly appeared and marched me off in double time, "Queeek march. One two, one two, one two." My poor little legs seemed to be going so fast I was practically running between the guard. Breathless, and horribly embarrassed. Desperately wishing I hadn't done it. Desperately wishing it wasn't me whose legs were hardly touching the ground. Desperately wanting to be "normal", back in the crowd, unsullied by such a shameful disaster. The guardroom door clanked behind me. I was locked up.

About an hour later, after the practice session had ended, Staff turned up at the Guardroom.

"Why ever did you do it Miss Wright? Why ever did you move?" I explained apologetically. Her eyes rose heavenward, bosom heaving as she sighed deeply. "Haven't you understood anything at all about Sandhurst? Well, I hope you've learnt your lesson now. What are you?" I thought it better to keep my lips shut in a tight, humble line, than venture to guess what I was. She was not really sympathetic. I'd broken a very basic rule. But after this nothing more was ever said about it by the DS.

"What's it like in the guardroom?" All the girls were agog to know. And very soon I became famous throughout the whole course. Whenever I met one of the men they'd always say, "Oh you're the one……….." I achieved my 15 minutes of notoriety.

April came, and the Senior Division was to pass out. HRH Princess Anne was to perform the inspection. We were rather excited. The passing out parade was a terribly smart affair, with the band, the horses, all the big wigs. And of course a real live audience of friends, relatives and guests of the academy. By now I'd learnt a lot more about outdoor kit, and I'd been completely bowled over by something called "heat pads". These were small, soft bags, (a bit like tea bags, and some larger), that when rubbed between the hands gave out heat. They had something very clever inside that was activated by the rubbing. I thought they were brilliant, and had taken to wearing them inside my gloves when we went out on exercise. The weather in April was quite cold still, and I decided that, as we would have to stand to attention for a long while on parade, I would pin a couple of these heat pads to my vest. To keep my core warm. What a great idea.

We were dressed and inspected, and marched onto the parade ground. The lovely horses alongside, the band playing stirring tunes. I guess the whole thing lasted about an hour.

Princess Anne is a wonderful woman. And when Princess Anne is called upon to inspect the troops at Sandhurst I can assure you she will inspect every single person on parade from the top of their cap to the tip of their boots. Most conscientious, she takes her time when called upon to perform this public duty. Wonderful woman.

About half way through I felt a tremendous heat on my chest.

"Gosh it's working well," I thought, congratulating myself. Smug. About three-quarters of the way through we had to stand to attention whilst Princess Anne went round inspecting us all. I wondered what would happen if she found a piece of fluff on a cap, or a smear somewhere. To my horror some poor chap a few rows in front of me passed out, and had to be dragged off. Apparently it was quite common, and nothing to worry about.

"God, I hope I don't faint," I thought suddenly feeling giddy. A deep breath. We were getting near the end of the inspection, and HRH was getting closer to my row, when realised I could smell something that could only be burning. And suddenly I distinctly felt a sharp stab of pain. On my chest.

"Ouch! What on earth was that?" I thought. I managed to adjust my position by a milli-fraction, and it stopped. But then it came back again. It was rather like a very sharp searing needle prick. Or as though my skin were touching something hot. And then it dawned on me. The awful realisation that the heatpad was overheating. As HRH drew closer I only just managed to avoid putting my hand to my mouth in horror. The heat pads were getting hotter and hotter. So was my chest. There was no air circulating down there to cool anything down. My chest was now cooking. I continued to stand to attention. Like a horrified statue. Unable to move, to Do anything. I was praying like I'd never prayed before that HRH would not be within roasting range when the first person to undergo spontaneous combustion on the parade ground at Sandhurst burst into flames.

At last her long inspection was over, and it was time for the Senior Division to follow the white horse, up the steps and into Old College. The traditional end to the passing out parade. Only those who had passed the course got to follow that horse. Wonderful stuff. But by now I was completely panic stricken. Time was running out. Although I had narrowly avoided involving HRH in one of the most bizarre "terrorist attacks" in the history of the British army, I swear I could now smell strong whiffs of smoke as my vest and then my blouse, and then my person itself, began to ignite. I tried to hold my chest in, rounding my shoulders surreptitiously, easing my clothes forward and away from the heat pad. Just in time we were marched – me now in real pain - off the square, round to the back of Old College. My sister came running up to congratulate me. I grabbed her hand and ran with her into the block, tearing at my clothes as I went.

"What on earth are you doing?" she shouted, alarmed.

"Getting rid of this," I retorted as I pulled the smoking pad out and we stared at the blackened hole smouldering in my M & S thermal vest.

"Thank you God. Just in time." I flopped down onto my bed. "If Princess Anne had delayed just a little bit longer she'd have been able to see me go up in flames," I explained to my horrified sister.

"Why ever did you do it?" She queried, in a disbelieving tone. "You don't change do you? Haven't they been able to teach you any sense here?"

Chapter 11 – The best parade

As the better weather arrived, so the course got more bearable. It was lovely to be up early now. We'd see brilliant sunrises, and I vowed that whatever happened later in life I'd always get up to see these still, fresh new starts, when the day feels as though its hanging in the air just waiting to begin. Before anything disturbed its peace.

We had more free time. To play tennis, go for more leisurely walks through the woods, across the great lawns, to discover the library, have impromptu parties down at the lake. We could even get out in the evenings if we got a pass, and my great friend Iain would come down occasionally and take me off to London for a really good night out. I'd feel insatiable for fun on these occasions, and after we'd driven up to Town, had a meal and a few drinks we'd go to a nightclub and dance and dance. But that was never enough. I felt I had to use up every moment of freedom, and poor Iain had to trawl around in the small hours, after the club had closed, to find somewhere else that was still open and would sell us a drink. Only by about 4 in the morning would I agree to try to find his car again and drive back. I just felt I really had to make the most of the opportunity. It felt so good to be out and with a man. A kind and generous-hearted man, funny too, who was both prepared to put up with my exaggerated need to party, and who put no demands upon me whatsoever. He was also important to me as a contact with my old life. My old me. Which was really the same as the new me. Just a bit more battered now. And he was also important to me because I really appreciated his taking the trouble to come down, and whisk me off in his sporty little number, in front of the other girls. That they saw me mattered. They saw that even though I was so much older, I could still interest a man. So I guess, bluntly, I used him. Even though I liked him enormously. I had a pact with myself by now. So many people had said,

"Oh joining the Army to find a man are you?" But I knew I'd joined the Army to get away from a man. I'd done this for me. Because I'd made such a mess of things, and I wanted to get away from the guilt. I'd made a pact with myself to get everything I could out of the Army in terms of a life experience, except a man. Life had seemed empty and I'd wanted to fill it. And I just wanted to really Do something. I didn't deserve, or want, any more serious relationships. I was going to be Independent.

Life certainly was full now, and still there was something to dread every day. Something to keep me on my toes. But fewer inspections now. And there was more fun. We'd all made firm friends. We felt deep respect for the DS and they seemed to be showing their more human faces now. Some of the girls were indulging in a spot of romance with the male cadets. Really it was a lovely place to be. I felt very privileged indeed to be there.

We continued to have our progress interviews, and although we weren't told too much other than whether we could stay on the course or not, we were congratulated if we'd done something well. We were even given a week's holiday. Not to go away on holiday of course, but to do some form of adventure training. I managed to get a week's sailing. I'd never been on a sailing boat before, only on a fishing boat at Bridlington with my uncle. So this was in truth quite an adventure. Fortunately one of the other girls on the boat did have some clue as to what to do with all those ropes, and fortunately she was a forceful character. I just did as I was told. Although by the second day I did get a bit sick of it. And a bit sick.

And so the months went by, until we had our final exercise. In North Wales. We had to climb Snowdon and camp on the mountain. I was in a group with Jemima so we were often helpless with laughter. And we had plenty to laugh about. The weather on Snowdon was pretty rough, and conditions at times treacherous. We still hadn't got the hang of those tents, and woke up in the early hours one morning in a huge cold puddle, with lashing rain and a howling gale, the canvas collapsed and flapping around our ankles. We had to run around quickly, trying to collect all our kit which was rapidly being washed away by large streams of water which hadn't been there the night before. This exercise was probably called Adventure Training Somethingorother. We then stayed in very basic, what I would have called temporary, accommodation. Although Tina assured me it was beyond her expectations, and I guess it could have been worse. And every day we had to tackle vertical cliff faces, traversing, abseiling, potholing, caving, canoeing, high wire trapeze tricks, aerial dives, and a horrible assault course with ingenious water features. There was something to terrify everyone. I guess this was where the friendships and mutual support were invaluable. The army staff were also brilliant. Patient for what seemed like hours. And with a great sense of humour. I'll never forget the sergeant who, to my astonishment, got me to traverse across the top of a huge sheer cliff-face. I knew that if I hesitated even for a second I'd freeze with terror and be there for hours. The trick for me was to keep going, and his encouragement and humour did just that.

Interestingly, and by all accounts "coincidentally", my parents were holidaying in North Wales at exactly the same time. Odd that. And I was given permission to meet up with them one evening. My mother was just so relieved to see me still alive.

Then came the greatest day of all. Our final progress interview with the DS. I was told I'd passed the course. I was told I'd be one of the cadets to pass out from the historic Old College parade ground, up those steps, following the white horse. I just kept hearing the words, seeing the image, over and over again. I'd done it. And again, not for the first time, I thought of my little office in Leicester Square. My first outing in those trainers. And the fateful set of circumstances that had led me to such a point in my life. I was told that our passing out parade would be held on the 8th August 1986. We were allowed to request up to 8 tickets for friends and relatives. My parents, sister and her boyfriend, and 4 friends. To my delight there were some spare tickets going, and so I was able to invite Harold, my old boss, and another work colleague and her brother, and 2 of my dearest friends from America too. I was so thrilled to think of sharing this special day with such special people.

At our final interview we were also told by the Commander what posting we were to be given. I'd been so wrapped up in Sandhurst that what happened afterwards had never been prominent in my mind. Of course I'd considered it but only too vaguely. And I rather fancied Hong Kong, or Cyprus. So did everybody else! We'd been asked, some weeks back, to give 3 preferences. But I realised they couldn't always accommodate our, rather naïve, wishes. I rather suspect they just had a jolly good laugh. So I really didn't know what to expect at all.

"You will be posted", began our Commander in a rather grand tone, "in the rank of Lieutenant," (all graduates left Sandhurst as a Lieutenant) "to The Second Battalion The Royal Green Jackets. To begin with as their Assistant Adjutant," she added. This was something I most certainly had not expected. And I was rather startled. And not a little afraid. All I could think was,

"Aren't they that crack infantry regiment. Very warry. I'm not crack, infantry or warry."

And then she continued, "This is the very first time ever that a woman has been posted with The Royal Green Jackets. It is quite an honour to have been selected. Well Done, Miss Wright."

I wasn't really taking this in. Was I supposed to agree that it was indeed an honour?

"Oh dear, will I?" was all I managed.

"You will, of course, be the only woman there." She said this with a finality. I was dismissed, but only after she had bestowed a warm smile.

I was really quite shocked. "The Royal Green Jackets?" I thought. "That elite infantry lot. They didn't take women. Did they? So why take one now? And why only one? And why me? What would I have to do?" It was so unexpected. Yet again, it struck me that fate had dealt another quirky blow. Just as I'd decided to give up men completely and for ever, I get posted to live amongst a battalion of them! As a lone female! My mind tried to remember all that the Commander had told me. It hadn't been much. But I was heartened to hear that they were posted in Warminster. That wasn't too far from home, in Nottinghamshire, if I needed a bolt hole. And my sister was in Guildford now so I could always run there. When I told Tina she was very impressed. So were the others.

"Ooh, aren't they known as "The Black Mafia"?" they said, much increasing my nerves.

My father when I told him was frankly astonished. But it just gave my poor old mum more to worry about.

"Infantry," she gasped. "What on earth will you be doing? Exercises all the time?" Not what I wanted to hear.

True to form I only really wanted concentrate on the most immediate events. And I threw myself into anticipation of them.

There was to be a ball too, on the evening of the 8th August. And again I was really lucky to be able to have more spare tickets. Lots of my friends could come, and I knew I wanted to invite Glenda. I could probably get hold of her through Luciano at the wine bar. I was sure she'd still be going there. After all it was her second-home. Or, in terms of time spent there, first.

How I looked forward to the Big Day. I guess it was like looking forward to a momentous, and very personal, celebration, rather like that wedding I'd never have now. All my friends and family would be around me to celebrate something wonderful in my life. And to look to the future. I could hardly wait. But I did feel very sad at the thought of splitting up from all those wonderful friends I'd made.

When the day dawned, and I did see it dawn, it was full of promise for fabulous weather. My kit spat on and polished ad nauseam, I could hardly breakfast. But fear of fainting on the parade square made me eat. I rushed back to the block from the cookhouse........not being marched there and back on this day. And there was my father, in the courtyard. Looking very handsome, smart, and happy. And terribly proud. I flung my arms around him.

"Thank you for coming. Thank you for coming early. I'd have burst if I'd had to wait to see you and mum any longer." We all hugged. Emotional. Proud. Choked. What a moment. Like I imagined a bride might feel. It couldn't have been any better.

We had a walk around and I chatted happily about the forthcoming events. Then more friends and my sister arrived. More hugs. Great excitement building up. Then I was called away to get dressed. To prepare. (No heat pads today.) And my friends and relatives took their seats in the Sandhurst Memorial Chapel for the service that would give thanks as the fitting start to our celebrations. It was a lovely service. Just the right touch. But I guess they'd been doing this for a long time. And they were just the right people to do it. Apparently the Sultan of Brunei, himself an ex-cadet at Sandhurst, would be taking the salute. And inspecting.

At last. Band, horses and us were ordered to begin the, for me, momentous march onto the parade square. Tina and I winked at each other, supporting each other to the end. I wanted it all to last forever. The tingle at the back of my neck, the feeling of utter happiness. The stirring music in tune with my pride in my achievement.

I don't know if we marched well that day. Everyone said we were brilliant. But it felt truly fantastic. I do know that my parents and friends sat on the edge of their seats and shed real tears. The whole atmosphere was gravely serious, utterly professional, timed to perfection, and euphorically joyous all at once. Magical. The stuff that all my dreams had been made of all those months ago. Life was sweet.

And when we followed that white horse up those steps, clattering into the Old College foyer, we shed tears too. Proud, happy. A tight group for the last time in our lives.

"I will always remember this as a very real consolation for never being able to experience my wedding day," I promised myself. "It makes up for it." And for my father I prayed it made up, in some small way, for not having had his day up the aisle, proud and happy.
Could he feel proud of me again?

Pulling ourselves apart from the great hugging heap we'd made, we dashed down the long stone corridor which stank of horse, and out into the sunshine to join our friends and our families. A grand lunch was to follow for all in Old College. Poached salmon, and strawberries. All the big wigs, all the DS were there, laughing and chatting with us and our family groups. Jokes shared, horrors remembered with great merriment. One by one we drifted away from the lunch party to collect our personal belongings and load them into our parents' cars. We were really leaving Sandhurst. The block felt sad, empty, echoing our goodbyes. But Jemima's parents, living close by in Camberley, had invited as many as wanted to go for tea at their house. My father and I went together, and stayed until it really was time to go, hanging on for as long as possible. And together.

Of course I had the ball still to look forward to, and around 7pm my sister, and all my friends turned up to party with me. I was wearing my Mess uniform, but one friend decided I'd look less stuffy if she decorated my hair with lots of those little flags they stuck in the cocktail cherries. I did look less stuffy. But a bit of a nerd. It was great to see Glenda again. She'd found herself a nice man, or a nice man had been lucky enough to find her, and she seemed really happy. First we drank champagne on the lawns before we went in to dinner. Then lots of dancing. Lots of fair-ground rides – horses and dodgems. The best fun. And then at mid-night a fantastic, spine tingling display of spectacular fireworks. Lots of cracks and big bangs. Lots of "Oooohs and Aaaaghs."

And then it was over.   Silence.   A collective disappointed "Ohhh......"   And people began to move away.

"That's it then," I thought.   And a cold shiver went through my whole body as I realised.   It was The End. The end of Sandhurst.   The end of the ambition.   The dream.   The end of all I'd wanted to achieve.   My eyes filled with water.   I tried to see friends in the crowd.   I couldn't see any one person.   The crowd was a blur as it moved away.   Moved away past me like a stranger now as I stood there, watching it, silently weeping.   Wanting it all to come back.

But of course I couldn't stop there.   I'd got to move away, and on, too.   A new door had been unlocked for me.   A great big wide door.   Opening onto another void. With the darkness of ignorance yet again beyond it. And was I prepared to go through that door?   Was I ready? Competent enough?   How could I possibly know if I wanted to?   But, in the Army there's not a lot of choice.

Chapter 12 – Reporting for duty

I had a couple of weeks leave before I was to report to a Battlesbury Barracks near Warminster in Wiltshire to join The Royal Green Jackets.   And I decided to spend it between my old haunts in London, and my parents" home in Nottinghamshire.

It was really nice to know that although I'd lived away from home for years I could still return there and receive invitations to parties from old friends.   And whilst I was on leave an invitation did indeed arrive, to a rather grand party to be held in Newark, a local town. One of my parents' acquaintances, a widowed lady of some substance, who was one of the main socialites of her very social village up the road, offered to lend me an evening dress. This was very kind because I really had nothing appropriate to wear. She sent several wonderful creations down to my parents' house for me to choose from, and we had great fun as I paraded from room to room in these luxurious gowns. Although the widowed lady was a couple of decades older than me she still had great taste, and a great figure, and I coveted all of her clothes.

At last I selected a white, close-fitting and low-necked dress that made me look a bit, (only a bit), like one of those Greek goddesses that you see painted on cheap imitation vases. But I was happy and that was all that mattered. And off I went, in my new figure and borrowed gown, to the party.

By very odd coincidence, (and doesn't life have this strange habit of throwing very odd coincidences every so often?), I met an army officer that evening. Before embarking on my mad adventure I had simply never met one before. Now they were coming out of my ears it seemed. He was very charming. And very attentive. Was it the dress I wondered? He asked me to dance. Several times. I enjoyed the attention. Flattered, and rather excited. It was at this point that a friend took me on one side and quietly explained that my army officer was engaged. And his fiancée was the rather pretty but miserable-looking girl frowning in the corner. The friend continued, "so, would you mind very much Gilli, disappearing to the loo for a good half-hour so that she can reclaim him."

I'd never seen myself in the role of a femme fatale

before. But there were a lot of things I'd never seen myself as before which I was becoming. And I was damned if I was going to retreat. If he preferred me to his fiancé could I help it? And it had been some time since I'd had the flattering attention of such a charming man. It was a rather lovely feeling. And it had got hold of me. As had the champagne and the posh frock. I'd passed out of Sandhurst as an officer and it wasn't my fault I was now bewitchingly attractive.

Tonight I was a Greek goddess. Could I help it if mere mortals fell at my feet?

My officer and I danced the rest of the night away, and then exchanged phone numbers. And I left with his assurances of a phone call in the morning keeping me all warm and wriggly in my tummy. I hadn't noticed what had happened to his fiancé, I didn't really care at this point, and my friends kept a tactful, probably disapproving, silence.

Over the next few days the phone rang many times of course, but never was it my army officer, and I was disappointed that my conquest was apparently so short-lived. And the episode unsettled me. What of my behaviour? What of my pact? Deep down in the bowels of my psyche was I really wanting a new man? Or was I simply having fun, using him as he'd used me? Did it only take a few glasses of champagne to turn my head to mush? Was I just on a high? How could I forget my crime? I wasn't sure about any of this, and I turned my attention to preparing for the great departure to Wiltshire. My mother and I went on a shopping trip with an enormous list of essentials; stand-bys, and treats for inevitable darker moments. Back to Newark. And as we came out of Marks and Spencer, there in the main road was my officer. Arm in arm with a very pretty girl. A girl I'd never seen before. Decidedly not the fiancé. My heart stood still for a moment. My face fell. Huh! So that was army officers was it? But it was no more nor less than I deserved.

I pondered long on this little cameo. I hadn't behaved well and I'd let my ego blow up to ridiculous proportions. Fuelled by the champagne and the expensive, bold outfit.

But it was quite a come down, I'd been duped. So had his fiancé, and probably lots before us. But I'd allowed myself to be duped so easily. I must be more careful. I was just off to live with a battalion of men! If just a little bit of flattery could hook my vulnerability so fully I must be more on my guard and be more determined. After all if I fell so easily for all the Green Jackets' charms I'd end up with no pride ever after, I'd be a complete laughing stock, commanding no respect and worse. Perhaps it was a good job it had happened - It was telling me something. I should listen.

As my leave dwindled away I wished I knew more about the Royal Green Jackets. Memories drifted into my mind about the horse, (was it Sefton?) and the bandsmen of the Green Jackets being bombed by the IRA in Regent's Park, back in 1982. Although I wasn't at all interested in the army I had been shocked and appalled at the time. And now I was going to join them. The feeling of unreality had set in again. Tina assured me that their officers were usually from public school backgrounds (major public schools), and usually had independent incomes (large ones). Some had titles. I hadn't met many of those types before. However, I was soon to start forming an opinion of them. Or at least of their Commanding Officer.

Whilst I was on leave, he took the trouble to

telephone my mother, (who was all of a jitter about her daughter joining an infantry battalion). He very kindly assured my mother that I would be looked after, and indeed that he himself would see that I was cared for properly. If she had any concerns about anything at all she was to make sure that she rang him personally. I heard her responding to this call. She was all coy and giggly. When she came off the telephone I was convinced that she'd just fallen in love again. I'd never seen a female so charmed. She fluttered her eyelashes at me.

"You'll be all right there Gilli," she declared. "If he's anything to go by. Ooh. Very. All right."

As the 2 weeks slipped past, I started to muse about these Green Jackets. I wished I'd asked for more information. I wished I knew what they were going to be like. Apparently I was to be their Assistant Adjutant. I wanted to know what this meant in more detail. I understood I was to work in Battalion Headquarters, but it was probably for the Commanding Officer and his Adjutant to decide on my exact duties when they met me and saw how I fitted in. I wasn't at all sure about being the only woman among a battalion of men.

"Why do they want a woman now?" I wondered. "Did they want a woman? Or was I part of some creeping policy or, worse still, experiment of equality in the forces?" It seemed a bit too token to be effective.

My parents and I mulled this over together.

"Just remember that although you'll feel strange being the only woman, and the first woman, that they will feel just as strange. They've got hundreds of years of tradition behind them. Tradition of being an all male set-up. It will be just as hard for some of them in some ways as it will be for you. They've probably been to all male schools. Might not have sisters. They might not all be ready for change. They might not want you. They might find it difficult having a woman living with them in their Mess. Be patient." That was what they said.

"Mmmm.....I just simply can't imagine any of it," was all I could contribute to this.

I'd had to pass my driving test whilst at Sandhurst. An officer, after all simply had to drive. My father and his friend, Hughie, had found a light blue second-hand Renault 5 for me, and I christened her "Coco." After Coco Channel, of course. I was terribly proud to have a car for the first time in my life – and I was 29! The morning for departure arrived. The car all packed up, I bid farewell to my parents and promised to give them a ring from the Officers' Mess, my new home, that evening.

"Don't forget, when you get fed up of it," shouted my father as the car nervously jolted down our road, "just give me a ring and I'll come and get you........"

"Huh!," I thought. "Now I've got to see it through to the bitter end. The old bugger."

And off I drove to Wiltshire. About a 7-hour journey the way I drove! Slowly and nervously. One hand on the steering wheel, the other clamped to my mouth. I needed another to bite some finger nails. As I progressed I thought non-stop about my destination.

"What would it be like? Who would be there? Who would meet me? What would I have to do? Would they be friendly? How should I dress? Who should I salute? Would anyone salute me? Should I use make-up? At all? How would we eat? Would I have to go on exercise straight away? Would I have to share a bathroom with the male officers? A toilet?" On and on. So many questions kept cropping up in my head. I knew none of the answers, and by the time Warminster started appearing on the signposts I'd worked myself up into a right fever pitch of alarm.

I'd been sent directions to the barracks, and they weren't difficult to find. I could see all the buildings, and playing fields, a cricket pitch, a driveway with a guardroom. There it was. Waiting for me. I'd arrived. And I drove straight past. No way did I feel like approaching that guardroom. I was plain terrified. So I just kept going, straight on. I could see the soldiers. What was I going to say to them? I tried to rehearse a little introduction...

"Hullo, I'm Lieutenant Wright, the new Assistant Adjutant. I'm not a proper soldier, I just happened to get through Sandhurst. Fluke really. Don't expect me to know anything, or be any good at anything. Could you direct me to the Officers' Mess please. Thank you."

I turned the car around, and drove back. And straight past again.

"I just can't do this," I explained to myself out loud. "Just can't." "Yes you can. You've got to. Come on. Do it." I tried to be cross with myself. To order myself like Staff had done. The car turned round, I approached again. I indicated to turn up the drive. The car turned in. And back out again. So sharply that Coco was almost on 2 wheels, and screeching her poor tyres.

"Well, that's done it." I told myself. "They were bound to notice that. Probably the most exciting thing that's happened all day. You've got to go in now. Or they'll think you highly suspicious, casing the joint, keeping on sailing past."

So I did. I drove up to the soldiers and even managed to wind down my window.

"Er, well, um er Hullo. My name's........." They were obviously expecting me. And had obviously guessed who I was by the 3rd or 4th time I'd driven past. They saluted smartly and directed me, very politely, very professionally, to the Officers' Mess. There was no turning back now. Gulp.

I drove, slowly, along a narrow road, past various buildings, past soldiers going about their business. What would I meet at the Mess I wondered? Nerves were jangling. I couldn't bite my lip anymore. I'd already made it too sore. There was a car park. I parked the car. Got out, legs a bit shaky. And walked to the front entrance. Inside this ordinary looking building an impressive sight greeted me. Huge oil paintings. Mostly of old soldiers going way back when. They looked down on me, disapproving. Waiting for me to offend them. There was a portrait of the Queen. Lots of polished silver gleaming. Everything spotless. And a large man in uniform. A couple of teeth missing. A mop of unruly light brown hair, and large nervous brown eyes. He looked terribly uncomfortable.

"Lieutenant Wright?" He queried. "The guardroom rang to say you were on your way. Er, um, I'll take you to the Colonel. Now. Follow me."

I realised that he was, if anything, more nervous than even I was, and I followed him back through the entrance, and down the road to another building. He fair shot up some stairs, indicated a door marked "Commanding Officer", and ran back down the stairs as quickly as he could, as though desperate to get away from something so extraordinary as a woman. Left all alone in this deserted corridor I knocked at the door.

"Come," said a pleasant voice, and I entered a large office, and met one of the best of men I was ever to have the good fortune to meet. His name was Lieutenant-Colonel Hugh de Blundell Hardwick-Dale.

What a handle. What a man.

"Hullo Gilli," warm and friendly as he leapt up to shake my soggy hand. "Please don't call me Sir. We try not to be pompous in the Green Jackets, and all my officers call me "Colonel". How are you? How was your journey? How are you feeling?" He indicated to me to sit down, and picked up a telephone to order some tea.

"I'm fine thank you S.., um Colonel." I lied. And then I decided I could be a bit more honest with such a warm human being, "Well, you know, a bit nervous actually."

"I'll tell you something," the good Colonel responded conspiratorially. "That was Sergeant Major Wolf who just brought you over here. He's responsible for the smooth running of the Officers' Mess. He's been an infantry soldier all his career. Warry sort of chap. He's been in a flat spin for weeks now expecting you. He's been in and out of my office several times a day just lately, asking what he should call you in the Mess, should they bring you a cuppa in bed in the morning, asking which bathroom you should use, and should he get in special soap. On and on. When he knew you'd arrived this afternoon he got straight on the phone to me. In a right panic. A jibbering wreck.

"She's coming, she's coming, what shall I do with her?".
And all that sort of thing. And it was only kind to
suggest he bring you straight over here to me while he
recovers from the awful shock of meeting you."

He grinned at me, and I laughed politely. More
nervous than ever now. I'd not thought too much about
the reality of sharing my bathroom with lots of male
officers. And where the soap had been. I'd not thought
about the Mess staff – all male. The tension was
beginning to build up. I started to feel queasy. Not even
cups of tea were going to ease this sort of tension.

"Well, off you go then now Gilli. Settle into the
Mess. And I'll see you in the morning. Come to my
office at 7 am and I'll introduce you to everyone here in
Battalion Headquarters. We hope you'll be very happy
with us, and never fear to come to me if you've any
problems you need help with. Don't worry if you feel
nervous or a bit strange at first. It would be quite
natural. Just remember, those that matter don't mind,
and those that do mind well, they don't matter do they?"
And I was dismissed. In the nicest possible way. But
dismissed. To go back to the Mess on my own. To find
my own way. I guess that was for the best. Thrown in.
Get on with it.

I found my way back, and went over to Coco. She
felt like my only friend. My only link with back home.
I took some of my stuff out of the boot and wandered
back into the Officers' Mess. Sergeant Major Wolf
appeared as if by magic. Had he been anxiously
watching out for my return? Dreading the hour as much
as I was? On seeing me he opened a door off the hall
and shouted at the top of his voice,

"Lance Corporal Black! Here! Now! Come and help the Assistant Adjutant with her kit." A very pleasant young rifleman appeared, smiled at me, and introduced himself. Warmly shaking my hand. I instantly liked him. He wasn't at all scared of me. Interested, yes. He took my bags and set off up the stairs. The Sergeant Major, feeling more safe in numbers, indicated I was to follow, "we'll show you your room ma'am. I hope everything will be satisfactory." As we went up the broad flight of stairs, a young officer came tripping down. He stopped and looked at me.

"This is the new Assistant Adjutant Sir," said Sergeant Major Wolf nervously.

"Oh Hi," mumbled the officer, and continued tripping.

"We're all a bit uncertain ma'am," declared the sergeant major. I nodded understandingly,

"...mmm, to be honest with you Sergeant Major so am I. More and more uncertain." And with that shared, we started to get more pally.

"Everyone calls me Wolfy ma'am. Don't bother with the Sergeant Major bit. Not while we're in the Mess."

My room looked pleasant enough. For an institution. I had a lovely view across some lawns and then fields. That made me feel at home. Then "Wolfy", with a discreet but rather proud "ahem," ceremoniously opened a door, obviously very pleased with himself.

"This ma'am is your very own lavatory." He was obviously thrilled to show it to me. "It was built specially for Princess Anne. When she came to visit last year. We had to provide a room for her to change in and, you know, and had to quickly build in a lavatory so she didn't have to go with the boys. Lucky for you."

Yes indeed. I was most grateful to Princess Anne and to her reserve in that department. So, not only had she nearly seen me go up in flames a few months ago, but now we had a lavatory in common.

"You'll still have to share the baths," he added nervously. Bringing me back down to earth.

"Oh, right. Yes. Thank you," I replied rather too heartily, hardly daring to imagine what this might mean, and not wishing to prolong this direction in the conversation.

Corporal Black got up all my things in no time, and very kindly trotted off to get me some more tea.

"Dinner is at eight ma'am. Will you be dining? It's not a black tie night. But smart." I hadn't thought this far ahead, and started to panic. How could I dine? In the Mess? Amongst all those strangers? All men? Would I be smart enough? But I'd got to get it over with some time.

"Yes, Corporal Black, thank you. I shall dine." I felt like the Queen. But the Queen when she's nervous. "I expect she must be sometimes," I mused as Corporal Black left me to it.

I tinkered around, unpacking slowly. Trying to decide what to wear for my great entrance. 8 o'clock was still some hours away. Perhaps I should go exploring. Find these bathrooms. I could hear doors opening. Shutting. Who was doing the opening, shutting? What were they like, these other officers? But I didn't go out of my room to find out. Dinner would be soon enough I decided as I concentrated on trying to get my room to look a bit more cosy. I wondered about calling the parents, but the phone in the room was only connected to the military net, and I didn't like to ask the operator for a civilian number.

And 8 o'clock did arrive. Too soon after all. I was dressed and braved stepping into the world outside my room. Down the stairs. I found the door to the dining room. I could hear people talking beyond it. I took a deep breath. And another. God, what would it be like on the other side of the door? What would they be like? Should I introduce myself? Would others introduce themselves? Another deep breath. Deeper. Heart fluttering. Oh, where were all my friends? Any one of them? I pushed the door. I went in. Entered. Trying not to look around. Trying to walk bravely without tripping up. Trying not to look stupid. The conversation didn't stop. No-one took any notice of me at all. I found a seat and sat down. My face flushing annoyingly. The conversation was all about shooting. I couldn't join in. One or two smiled at me when I caught their eye. But that was about all. I wasn't made to feel out of place, different, or new. No-one drew attention to me at all. Everything carried on, as I guessed it did most evenings. In fact, everything carried on as though I wasn't there.

After dinner we took coffee in an ante room. The Mess staff waited on us. It was luxury really by anyone's standards. But again, no-one said anything to me. I began to wonder if my nose was terribly dirty, or if I was giving off a rather bad smell. I fled as soon as I'd drunk the coffee. Scalding my tongue in my haste. Back up to my room. To ponder my long-anticipated meeting with my fellow officers, and to worry over the whole day's momentous events. I'd brave entering the bathroom in the morning. I'd had enough for one day. The last thing I felt like meeting was one of them, possibly even naked, in the bath. Gosh my imagination was running riot! I realised that all this was rather sad because it was an opportunity that had never come my way before, meeting naked officers, and it seemed a shame not to make the most of it. But, right now, I didn't really want to meet an officer dressed either.

At least I'd got here. Safely. At least I'd made a start. A start on what I had little idea.

Chapter 13 – Settling In

When the alarm rang the next morning I sincerely wished myself back in my little office in London. My father had always threatened to buy me out of my commission if I were ever posted anywhere in the slightest bit dangerous. Would he classify sharing my bathroom with lots of male officers as "the slightest bit dangerous"? I wondered. I had the distinct feeling that I was a fish out of water here. In fact a fish out of water and riding a bike. I belonged here about as much as I belonged in a treacle pudding. And I felt about as welcome as that proverbial "fart in an astronaut's suit". This thought cheered me up no end. I chuckled aloud. And I wished Billy Connolly was one of the officers here. Just to keep these one liners going all day long. I needed them.

I decided to brave the bathroom, just down the

corridor. As I went inside I could hear someone splashing in one of the baths enclosed in a cubicle. What was a girl to do? It seemed risque to me to get into the one other bath, in the other cubicle, which was separated only by a thin tin wall. A thin wall which did not go all the way to the ceiling. There was a big gap. Neither did it go all the way to the floor. Another big gap. So it was only a band. A paper thin band of metal sheet. I quickly left the bathroom, trying not to panic I fled as quietly as I could. But I'd got to do it sometime. I'd got to wash! So I waited, sweating in my room, until I was absolutely sure the bathroom was empty and then I took my chance. I quickly leapt into one of the baths, and as I did this I almost said,

"So There!" I was pleased with my bold step.

I'd never tried to wash myself in silence before. But, at first, I didn't want to make any sound of splashing, or anything else. I was so acutely aware of being overheard. But then, instead I decided to make it snappy. And then, suddenly I heard the sound I had been dreading. Somebody came in. I froze. And all of a sudden a friendly voice said,

"Hullo, nice morning isn't it? How are you settling in?" Again, I froze. Should I reply? I'd never had a conversation with a strange man whilst taking a bath before.

"Well," I responded uncertainly.

"Good." Came the voice again, completely confident, still very friendly.

Aghast I said, "How did you know it was me?"

"Well," came the pleasant reply, "you have such a lightness of touch. Any of the blokes would be far more noisy. You see."

"Oh," I blushed. I wasn't sure I did see. Exactly.

Safely back in my room I realised I'd no idea who I'd been talking to. But he had, of course.

Breakfast was pretty much as dinner before, no-one took much notice of me. This was my first day, and to mark the occasion I'd donned my uniform. Something in me, I'd no idea what, had made me put on my bright pink lipstick. It was outrageously bright pink, called, I think "Searing Eyeball Pink". Or it should have been. But wear it I had to. I was quite sure it couldn't be classed as regulation, and certainly not in an infantry battalion. And off I tripped, back to Battalion HQ, and the Colonel's office with my badge of defiance screaming from my lips.

"Good morning Gilli," he was all charm. "Good morning Colonel." I was determined to be cheerful. "How are you feeling today? Settling in?"

"Oh yes, Colonel," I lied. "It's great." He was obviously no fool.

"Is it?"

I would not give in, and repeated, "Yes." Compounding my lie.

"Well," he said, obviously not going to argue. "Come and have a tour of Battalion HQ." And off we went. First we met the Chief Clerk who was polite and ponderous, his nose slightly red at the end giving him a look of a toy from long-forgotten "Noddy" stories. Then the Regimental Sergeant Major who was very smart, small, chipper, cheeky with dark sparkling eyes dancing with fun. We exchanged wise cracks, and I knew I'd found an ally. Thank God because if the RSM was not on my side I might as well go home. Here was a man willing to share a joke, more than willing by the look of him. We took an instant liking to each other.

Then on to the Paymaster. He was not a Green Jacket, but from the Army Pay Corps. His name was Jerry Quick. His office was small, more like a cubby hole, made smaller by his hanging a huge Japanese umbrella from the light bulb. He had enormous whiskers, that he bristled. And he had a large glass jar of brightly coloured sweets on his desk. Jerry was obviously as mad as a hatter. And I loved him straight away. Finally, oh dear, the Adjutant. From the moment I walked into his office - his office that he'd got to share with me from now on – I felt the cold draught. No, rather it was a strong breeze. He was stiff and I knew straightaway that he was resentful of my presence. He was studiously careful not to tell me anything that might be useful to me. His name was Robert, (could never be "Rob", "Bobbie", or "Bob"), Captain Robert Carlton-Hoe. It seemed to me that he was ambitious, and perhaps unprepared to work with a woman. A woman whom, he had heard, had held a good job in London before going on to do well at Sandhurst. Was I to be considered a threat? And female to boot.

The Colonel cheerfully left me to my induction with Robert. But Robert was not really prepared to talk to me for longer than 2 minutes at a time. At the end of each 2-minute burst he had to recover, by turning his back on me and burying his head in his in-tray.

"Here," he just about managed to utter at last, "get on with this would you." "This" turned out to be a long list, which he wanted typing out on the old manual typewriter in alphabetical order. I was quite sure he'd invented the task, to demoralise me, but I got on with it. And when it was completed he mumbled, "OK," and dismissed me back to the Mess, saying there was no more work left for me to do.

I sauntered back to the Mess. A long afternoon and evening ahead of me. Perhaps I should take myself off for a walk across the fields. It was a pleasant day, and I ought to keep up some sort of fitness, I'd nothing much else to do.

"Hullo," said a voice. I looked up to see a pleasant, slim, young officer, with gold-rimmed glasses beaming warmly at me. He was wheeling a bicycle along.

"Hullo," I replied returning his smile.

"I'm Michael MacGowen," he introduced himself, "how's your first day?"

"I'm not really sure yet, well, you know, it's OK so far really."

"Good. Any problems or questions do let me help." And with that he mounted his bicycle and, whistling as he went, disappeared.

"What a nice man," I thought, and I continued into the Officers' Mess. As I crossed the hall a man was descending the stairs. A shortish man with a shiny bald head, except for two patches of very blonde hair to either side. He had piercing blue eyes, that held me in their gaze. He had jodhpurs on, and knee-length black boots. I couldn't help staring back at him, he reminded me so much of the German officers you see in war films. It gave me a funny feeling inside.

"Good afternoon," snapped the character. I hesitated.

"Good afternoon," I mumbled back. And he'd gone. "Who on earth was that?" I wondered.

I didn't have to wait too long to find out. He was at dinner that evening. And he wasn't at all pleasant.

"Aha, the Assistant Adjutant is gracing us with her company," he snarled as I entered the dining room. I bristled. I had definitely taken a dislike to this man, and definitely didn't want to enter any conversation with him.

"Good evening," I managed to say, directing it at no-one in particular. Dinner progressed, the food as always was excellent, the service polite, considerate. Delightful really. But the Aryan character had decided he wasn't going to let go.

"So, we have a new Assistant Adjutant, has she settled in? Does she know what a tank is yet?" It appeared I was his quarry. It was understandable in some ways, I was new, I was a female, I was out of place. It was also unkind and immature. I realised he wanted to break me in some way. I couldn't get those old war films out of my mind. I decided to ignore him, and was relieved that the others ignored him too. I was left alone for the rest of the evening. No-one said anything else to me at all.

The next day I bumped into the Aryan in Battalion HQ. Literally. "Look where you're going Assistant Adjutant," he snarled. I shot him a dark look. The darkest I could shoot, and in as dignified a fashion as possible disentangled myself from him, turned my back on him, and slowly walked to Robert's office, my spine tingling with discomfort as I did so.

"Who is that man? You know, he's blonde but almost bald. Blue eyes. He seemed to arrive here yesterday," I asked Robert.

"Karl Theodore. Company 2ic. Just got back from a course." He didn't look up.

"Karl Theodore?" I replied astonished. "So he is German then?"

"Yes." Robert had had enough of having to converse with me. But I was intrigued.

"What's a German doing in The Royal Green Jackets? The British Army?"

"Family connection," snapped Robert. "Haven't you got any work to do this morning?" And that was as far as I got, for now. Family connections seemed to do it.

One day as I braved yet again trying to start a conversation with Robert I asked him a burning question.

"Why does no-one talk to me in the Mess?" Stiff at being addressed so directly he took a deep breath. To try to lessen his pain. I was obviously such an infliction.

"We're not the kind who make friends with strangers," he explained "We wait to find out what sort they are first."

"Oh," I responded cheerfully, "I wonder what sort I'll turn out to be." And that was that.

The following week I learnt that Michael MacGowen was to leave the Battalion.
He'd been posted elsewhere. I was saddened by this, He'd seemed so very kind, and rather interesting.

And my relationship with Robert improved not one iota as the weeks went by. I longed to get away from him, and frequently did. To the RSM''s office, or to Jerry's where we'd laugh heartily about my latest faux pas.......... and there was always a latest faux pas to laugh about.

As Assistant Adjutant I had various tasks; I had to sort out the orderly officers' duty rotas for my fellow subalterns. This was always a headache as no-one ever wanted to do orderly officer, especially the week-end duties which meant staying around all week-end when most had left for their country or London homes. I did feel that sorting out the orderly officer duty rota was made especially difficult for me because Robert would, under no circumstance whatsoever, allow me to take my turn at being orderly officer. I was a woman. I was not really part of the battalion, and could never be.

I did so want to work at being accepted by the other officers, and of course by the Riflemen. And it felt really uncomfortable ordering my peers to do their share of duties when I never did a single one myself. I suspected that Robert didn't want me to be accepted. I suspected that he was nervous of my doing anything well and taking any credit away from him. That had to be part of the reason why he wouldn't allow me to do anything other than the most basic of tasks? Or perhaps he just wasn't ready to accept me. He wanted to wait until he'd decided what sort I would turn out to be. When I pleaded with him to give me something to do he would reply airily,

"Yes, of course. Telephone so-and-so, and let them know I'll be telephoning them later." He really was the limit.

Eventually Fate stepped in to help me a little. There was one week-end when I just simply couldn't find any subaltern in the whole battalion who could actually do the duty. They all seemed to have reasonable excuses; parties in Town; long-arranged shoots on their country estates, girlfriends visiting. They'd been pretty good up to now at helping me out, and there was no-one I wanted to press into giving up their week-end. Could this be my chance I wondered?

I went off to consult my good friend the RSM, and explained the situation to him.

"You know, RSM," I began, "I really would feel better if I did my fair share of duties. The Adjutant is flatly against it, and I don't want to go behind his back. However, it just doesn't seem right that I insist all the other subalterns do their turn, and I never do my turn. But it's come to a bit of a crunch. This week-end I mean. There really isn't anyone who could do the duty. That is... well.... except me. I could. I'm the only subaltern who could do it this week-end without sacrificing something special. What do you think?"

"The Adjutant's against it you say Ma'am?"

"Flatly. Won't hear of it. But perhaps you could persuade him of the sense of it. It would mean there was another junior officer willing to do their share, and take some of the burden off the others. I can't see the harm in it. That's if you could explain to me exactly what I'd have to do?" I wondered what he would say. Perhaps he might think there would be a problem if the riflemen and the Senior Warrant Officers didn't accept my authority.

"I think you should do it," he said. "After all as the Assistant Adjutant you have to tell an awful lot of people what to do. It would undoubtedly look better if you were prepared to take your fair share. It would help the others to accept you, and to integrate you better. I'll talk to the Colonel about it, I'm sure he'd see the point. But you're right, you can't go behind the Adjutant's back. Leave it to me."

The Colonel, bless him, obviously had no problem and supported me wholeheartedly, and I was duly instated as the Orderly Officer for that week-end. I was delighted, and several of the younger officers thanked me for getting them off the hook. I began to feel there was hope. When the Friday afternoon came around I felt both very nervous, and rather excited at the prospect of being in charge for a whole week-end.

It all felt terribly real suddenly. The responsibility was awesome. I spent ages polishing my shoes and buttons, ironing my kit, flattening my hair under my cap, until at last, heart beating fast, I accompanied the Battalion Orderly Sergeant to mount the guard that evening. Would the Riflemen accept my authority? This was the first time ever that a woman had mounted the guard in a Royal Green Jacket battalion. I felt quite emotional, and proud, and tears sprang to my eyes as the duty Bugler played the Last Post and the Regimental colours were lowered in the evening sunshine. I was relieved that the BOS had shouted the commands this time because my mouth had gone all dry.

After this I followed the BOS, rather shakily, into the Guardroom to inspect the prisoners, and was frankly astonished and horrified at how pristine and dead neat all their kit was. Still I suppose they had enough time to get it like that. The Guardroom floor was so highly polished that I fair skidded up to one prisoner and only just managed to stop as our noses were about to rub. No-one laughed. No-one even smiled and, despite my nerves, I was determined too to remain solemn and dignified.

My meal was cooked in the Mess by one of the Mess staff. Apparently I could have whatever I liked over the week-end because I was the only officer there. The only person there. In that huge building. I munched away in reverent silence at the huge dining table, all those famous past members of the Mess staring down at me, thoroughly disapproving, through their gilt frames. I silently bet that a portrait of Robert would hang there one day looking haughty and cross.

It was odd going upstairs to sleep in the Orderly Officer's bunk, the phone by the bed. Waiting to ring, as I dreaded it might, with some urgent message for the responsible officer. What would I have to face I wondered? Who might want What? I really couldn't imagine. I just hoped no-one would want anything. At all.

It was the middle of the night, I was all alone in the huge Mess. It wasn't easy to relax and fall to sleep. I was aware of the big, dark, empty spaces out there beyond the locked door, and I kept remembering the silly stories some of the younger offices had told me about the Mess being haunted by some clanking being. The wind seemed to have got up and I was disturbed by the odd creaking and groaning noises I felt sure were not natural. I wasn't at all sure why I'd volunteered to do this. Robert was right. I was a girl and I was scared. Eventually, exhausted, I fell into a light sleep. But not for long, something far away disturbed me, and I woke up with a start. I was suddenly wide awake, alert, tense and straining to hear, to understand why I was so suddenly so afraid. And then, in the darkness, a resounding "Bang!". Followed by another loud explosion. Followed by glass shattering all around. Then eerie silence.

My heart was thumping its way out of my chest. I was shaking so much that I barely had control of my hands. I fumbled to reach the light. It didn't respond. Pitch blackness. I could now hear howling for God's sake. Another loud explosion. More glass shattering, this time in my room. My God, it was my window that had smashed. Who? What the hell was happening? I felt real fear then. Were we under attack? My body, shocked, had stopped breathing. Then, out of this unfamiliar chaos I could hear a very familiar sound. The phone was ringing. Loudly, urgently. I couldn't locate it at first and fumbled around desperate for some human contact. "Please don't stop ringing. I'm here and I need help." At last my fingers found it and I managed to hold it up to my ear, hands trembling.

"Is that the Orderly Officer?" A calm, strong voice.

"Yes," I managed to say weakly, trying to sound more in control as I remembered my awful new status. But silently I was in dread, "...don't ask me to help you, I need someone to come and help me," was all I could think, "and get me out of here bloody quick. Please."

"The alarm's ringing in the Armoury." It was a statement of fact, but the voice seemed to await my response, my instruction.

"Oh Bloody Hell." I spluttered. Really helpful. But by now I was totally panic-stricken. It must be a terrorist attack? They were after the weapons store? And apparently I'm in charge! Me! I tried to clear my head. I could still hear glass smashing in the corridor, and did not dare to imagine what was going on up there. Just a few yards up there. Just a few yards from me, alone in the pitch black.

I must get out of here. Now, alive.

"Tell the Battalion Orderly Sergeant to meet me outside the Armoury. In two minutes time," I whispered hoarsely. This was a thought that gave me hope. In two minutes time I could be out of here and safe with the Battalion Orderly Sergeant.

"And Corporal," I added quickly, "there seems to have been some explosions in the Officers' Mess. Make sure it's out of bounds until we find out more." I slammed down the phone and pulled on my clothes, stuffing my hair under my beret with shaking fingers. No time to find the basin to clean my teeth or wash my face. I stood at the locked door summoning up all my courage to unlock it and pull it open. What was, who was, beyond? In a moment my desperation to be out of there overwhelmed all my other emotions and I grabbed at it and ran out blindly. All was pitch black. I could see nothing.

I struggled down the corridor, horrible fear urging me to run. I kept bumping into things, but eventually, thank God, down the staircase and out into the night. Blackness all around, rain pelting down in chunks. Within seconds I was soaked to the skin. The howling wind made me gasp as it nearly blew me off my feet. I struggled blindly down to the Armoury, holding onto my sodden clothes for fear that they, with me inside, would be swept up and off into the night. I'd never experienced anything like it.

I hadn't seen the weather forecast for that week-end. Even if I had I don't think it would have warned me of what was to come. Michael Fish was to become famous for playing it down, for this was October 1987, and we were all in for a shock.

The BOS was waiting for me.

"Hullo there, Sgt Wilson, good to see you," I shouted with what little breath I had left, trying to make myself heard above the noise of the wind and rain. Relief like an instant pain killer to see that marvellous, competent person. "What's to report?"

"We've checked the Armoury Ma'am. Nothing missing. Nothing tampered with. There are several alarms going off around the barracks. It's fairly certain it's the wind that's triggered it. We seem to be having a hurricane wouldn't you say ma'am?" I could feel his efficiency, his control, and attempted to smile back at him. I'd never felt more relieved in my life. Oh, just a hurricane then. How wonderful.

"That would seem to make sense of everything," I screamed back. "Thanks Sgt. Let's go to the Guardroom, get a full picture of what's going on where. And a cup of tea."

I felt so much better now. Sergeant Wilson was so very able, and pleasant. He seemed to have everything under control already with his calm, intelligent good sense. We fought our way to the Guardroom. Once inside, in the dark, I noticed how quiet it seemed. Out of the weather which was howling, and screaming and beating away outside. I listened to the full report, and it seemed that the wind had smashed its way through several window panes.

So that's what I'd heard in the Mess. Several trees had blown down, but the full extent of the damage wouldn't really be seen until the morning when we had some light. There were no casualties – just lots of drama. Eventually, after several checks, and further reports we went back to our beds for what little remained of the night.

Only when I went round the camp in the first light of the next day did I understand the extent of the havoc wreaked by that storm. Later to be known as "the Great Storm of „87." What an introduction to Orderly Officer duties. Trust me!

Of course I had my share of other regular duties. They also took some getting used to. Robert had had to explain these duties to me, and he obviously hated having to do so. He used as few words as possible, and as little contact with me as possible and, as a result, I often got the wrong end of the stick. I remember my very first duty.

"Look," said Robert impatiently, "you need to go to the MTO's office. Find the corporal in charge, and tell him you've come to do the POL check. He'll understand, and do the rest automatically. Do this at least once a week. Sometimes early morning, sometimes evening. Vary it, so you take them by surprise each time."

"Thanks," I replied always determined to be polite and cheerful. "Um what does MTO stand for?"

"Don't they teach you anything at Sandhurst these days? Motor Transport Officer of course," he snapped. Thus far enlightened I didn't really want to ask what all the rest of it meant. I had no idea really what I was supposed to do, but Robert had made it sound straightforward, and I had rehearsed what I had to say to the corporal in charge. I got up early next morning, and before breakfast toddled off to the MTO's office. Just as Robert had said I found the corporal in charge.

"Morning ma'am," he saluted as he jumped up. Good, I'd obviously surprised him.

"Good morning Corporal Jones," I began, feeling rather important. Determined to look confident. I continued. "I've come to do the PLO check. Proceed please." The corporal looked me straight in the eye. Not a twinkle

"Sorry ma'am. We've none of those here." I was confused. It flashed through my mind for a fraction of a millisecond that Robert might be playing a trick at my expense. But that was ridiculous, of course. The poor chap simply wasn't capable of playing tricks. I was determined to keep showing my confident front.

"Alright Corporal Jones. Thank you. Carry on." And back I went to the Mess for breakfast, trying desperately to make sense of the whole episode. But I couldn't.

Later that morning, sitting in what I would always think of as Robert's Office, the RSM came bustling in.

"Ma'am a word please. In my office please. Now." I jumped up and followed him across the corridor. "What's this I hear about you searching for terrorists at the crack of dawn? Always inform me first if you suspect anything of that nature on my patch." He looked furious. I was appalled. What had I done? Then, to my complete relief his face broke into a broad, cheeky grin. "Corporal Jones of the MTO's office informs me you went to check for PLO this morning," he reminded me.

"Yes I did RSM. And Corporal Jones told me there were none," I replied.

"Well, thank God for that," continued the RSM, "we've got lots of POL though." He burst out laughing. Roared his head off. I still wasn't with it. "POL," he shrieked wiping tears from his eyes, "you were supposed to be checking the levels of petrol, oil and lubrication. Making sure it tallied with the books. That's something quite different you know from the Palestine Liberation Organisation." At last I understood. Of course I'd have to brave going back to see Corporal Jones next day, and do the thing properly. How I looked forward to that.

This wasn't the only mess I blamed Robert for. I'd only been with the battalion for a few days, and I was still trying my limited best to impress, to show I was competent and up for anything they threw at me. Suddenly, out of the blue, like a poisoned dart fired from a gun, Robert asked,

"How would you like to go parachuting?"

Well, I knew that the very last thing on God's earth, let alone off it, that I ever wanted to do was parachuting. But I wasn't going to say that. I wasn't going to let him know that. So I lied through my teeth.

"Oooh, love to." "After all," I was thinking to myself, "I'll never actually go. I'll be able to find some plausible excuse later." But Robert had landed his fish,

"Good. Right then" came his brusque reply. "You're booked in next week. Taking 20 riflemen down to Headcorn in Kent. Here's the paperwork." I was horrified. Just like that? I took the wodge of papers from his outstretched hand, convinced my face was the same white colour. "It'll give you a chance to get to know some of the riflemen better," he continued with a smirk on his face.

"Yes," I murmured weakly, "that will be lovely."

So I had a whole week to live in absolute dread of my life. I kept looking up at the sky, watching planes flying around and wondering why anyone would be allowed to jump out of them. I was also worrying about my recently-discovered fear of heights. Under normal circumstances that week, like every week here, would have dragged on. Not at all, it flew by, and I suddenly found myself in the back of a 4 tonne lorry in full combat kit, with 20 strange riflemen.

"Move up ma'am," said one cheeky one.

"Fancy a sweet ma'am" offered another. At least they spoke to me. Actually, by the time we reached Kent I felt like I had 20 new friends. It was immediately evident why the Royal Green Jackets are known as "thinking riflemen". They were intelligent and good-humoured. A really lovely bunch. Some of them were just as nervous about doing the jump as I was – they'd been ordered to go as part of their Adventure Training but most were determined to be brave and entertaining while they were at it.

And so, had Robert, actually rather cleverly and generously, done me a favour?

The accommodation block at Headcorn wasn't luxury by anyone's standards but I didn't expect much these days. It'd keep me warm, dry, fed and washed and I had some privacy. The training started pretty much straight away. Two army physical training instructors, PTIs shouted at us all day long, "Go, go, go," getting us to jump off things about 3 foot high and to roll over as we landed. It all sounded terribly easy, but it was immediately obvious I was not one of life's naturals at any of it.

"Ma'am you're too stiff. You'll break something." I was told too often.

"Probably the ground," cracked some wit.

And so we went on for about 2 days. And I hoped it would go on forever. I hoped I'd never be considered talented enough at this jumping and rolling to ever do the real thing. But sadly it wasn't like that, we were hauled on to the next stage - having to pack our own parachute. This I found totally unacceptable. I knew I had no-one to rely on but myself as I leapt from the plane and sped through thin air. But any shred of confidence I might have had would be completely evaporated if I knew that I'd also packed my parachute. There was no way I could contemplate this.

Fortunately the army had twigged to my incompetence in the direction of packing parachutes too, and in the end I was given one pre-packed by an expert. Thank God.

On the day of the jump we had to get up terribly early........ "to catch the right conditions" should they evilly occur. The 21 of us sat around on benches outside the huts. All kitted up. Waiting in dread to be told if these special conditions were apparent. The little aeroplane straining to get up there. We must have looked a pathetic lot, every shade of green was apparent in our faces. The strain of waiting a very particular torture.

"What made you want to do a parachute jump ma'am?" Asked one rifleman.

"I've no idea at all right now Rifleman West," was all I could reply. "Let's talk about our favourite episodes of "Star Trek" instead." We spent the whole of that day sitting on those benches, waiting for the order. It never came. And at last we were allowed back inside for some supper, and told to be back at the crack of dawn, seated on our benches to wait again. I didn't sleep a wink that night. I spent it leaping from various positions out of various aeroplanes, time and time again, going over everything as I lay fretting. How on earth had I got myself into this one?

The next day we waited all morning, anticipation working horribly on us. Thank goodness the riflemen had such wonderful, down to earth humours. In our tense states we really needed the release of laughter, and they did keep up the wise cracks. In that sense, I was grateful to Robert. I did feel that I'd got to know some of the riflemen, and they were definitely worth getting to know. Robert had indeed done me a favour.

Then, about 4 o'clock that afternoon, the PTIs came running over.

"We're on," they shouted to us. "Get over here." Feeling very sick, I wobbled over there, knees weak. No-one uttered a word. All deadly serious now. The sickness welled in and out of my stomach as we climbed on board the little plane, seven of us going at a time. I had decided that as the only officer, and the only female, I would go with the first batch. Ostensibly to set an example, in truth to get it over with. Couldn't hang about. Mustn't think about it. We sat crouched in the back of the plane, having to shout anything we needed to say at the top of our voices. With the door to the aeroplane wide open we were almost deafened by the noise which seemed to affect my heart now beating so fast it became one continuous beat. Apparently I was to jump fourth out of the seven. Oh Lord, I'd no strength at all in my limbs, they'd gone completely limp. We were lined up by the open door.

"Don't look down" a PTI screamed at us. Too late. I'd looked. Oh my God. The ground, the fields, so far away, so far down. It all began to swim around in my head.

"Go-Go-Go" screamed the PTI to the first rifleman. No hesitation. He'd gone, gone, gone. Leaving an empty space we had to fill.

"Don't look," came the scream again as our horrified eyes followed his plummet towards the ground.

"Go-Go-Go," came the scream again. Our man hesitated for a fraction. I saw the terror on his face and felt sure I'd be sick now. I felt sure he would be sick too but he wasn't, he jumped. The next jumped too. Then it was my turn. I could feel the icy wind rushing through the door. Pushing me back. The noise of the engine. Deafening. A ringing in my ears.

"Go-Go-Go," came my order. I braced myself. Not to be seen to hesitate, not as the only officer, the only woman. So I jumped. The shock of feeling nothing beneath my feet. Beneath my body. The shock of the freezing cold slipstream literally taking my breath away. A horrible sharp intake of the cold air. Freefalling. Spinning so fast everything was a blur. Gasping and spluttering I seemed to know nothing. I completely forgot my training and that I was supposed to check various vital, perhaps life-saving, things.

All of a sudden my descent was interrupted as I seemed to get pulled back upwards with a violent jerk.

"What the hell was that?" I panicked. Oh, I'd also forgotten all about the parachute opening!

After that it was a much more leisurely descent, and I kept telling myself to try to enjoy it, to try to appreciate the view because I was never, ever, going to do this again. But that was useless, I was still in shock and not enjoying anything at all.

And then, suddenly, I hit the ground. Hard. Ouch! I landed in a painful heap. All I could think was,

"Never, ever again." I spent a while just lying there. Getting my breath back. Assessing the damage. I realised I was shaking. My God, I'd done it! I was back down. For good. Eventually, slowly I got up and began to gather my parachute with still-trembling fingers, and I made my way, slightly staggering, over to the meeting point. I'd landed about a million miles away from where I was supposed to, and it was a long walk with all that heavy material. I tiptoed through the cowpats. Plentiful, large and fresh. But I felt that I'd done something so special that I ought to have been collected and driven back in triumph. To a fanfare. But it wasn't like that at all. I had to stumble my way across fields, my arms full of spent parachute. Warily navigating through the steaming cow pats. Thanks a bunch. When at last I made it to the meeting point I was handed my "Jump Report". It read as follows:

"<u>Lieutenant Wright</u>

Exit:-   Weak

Descent:-   Messy.   Arms and legs everywhere. Right hand went straight to the reserve."

"Oh," I sighed. The wind completely taken out of my sails. And did I want to have another go? I didn't even bother to reply as I staggered, legs still wobbly, off the field.

Eventually I made it back to the Mess very late that night. Exhausted and still shaking, but glad to be alive. I slept the sleep of the dead though, and next morning, refreshed, fairly tripped into breakfast.

"So did you jump?" Enquired one of the officers.

"What, parachute? Oh yes, of course," I replied airily.

"Did you really? Jolly well done." And everyone started congratulating me and asking what it had been like.

"But haven't you all done it?" I asked somewhat amazed.

"Oh no. Wouldn't get me up there and jumping out of a plane. Unnatural. Madness."

Yet again, I wondered why I'd had to do it then. But at least they were talking to me now.

Chapter 14 – Making Friends

One evening, just before dinner, there was a knock at my door. "Come in," I called. And in walked Michael Rounds, one of the younger officers, with his lively springer spaniel "Boots" who went everywhere with him. I made a fuss of Boots who was always desperate to play.

"How are you finding living in this Mess full of men

then?" Asked Michael straight to the point. Before I could reply he explained that he had a sister, and had been thinking lately how he'd hate his sister to be in my position.

"Why?" I wanted to know.

"Well, I think it must be very lonely. You've no-one really to talk to." I had to agree to this, I was lonely, dreadfully lonely at times. I kept up a cheerful façade, out of pride. I didn't want anyone to see how so alone I felt. My parents telephoned of course, my sister too, and my friends, but amongst all these men I was acutely aware that there was no-one „special. So, by joining the Army, I hadn't escaped my singleness. Indeed it stuck out more than ever now.

Here I was, 29 years old, very much single, and suddenly embarking on a career in the Army of all things. To my fellow officers I knew it seemed odd. They'd definitely not met anything like it before. All of their girlfriends were young, socially well-connected, confident, and well-heeled. They all thought I was odd too, or more importantly I felt they thought I was odd. They must have wondered what had made me do this. Why was I there? And I would have found it impossible to tell them.

My world of only a year ago seemed so far away that it hardly existed. These men moved in a different world, one to which I felt I could never belong, and those that were married, living in quarters, were the same. A different social stratum and a different view of things. But there were compensations like finding some exceptionally nice people around, funny people too, and things were definitely beginning to thaw a little.

Michael had just come to visit me. This was a new departure – visitors. I explained that I understood that it was difficult for everyone. Not everyone in the battalion could be pleased to have me, a woman, around. Michael looked at me, as if weighing me up, then,

"You can always talk to me you know. Treat me as a younger brother if you like."

I was rather overwhelmed by this simple but generous, and touching offer, but before I could thank him he'd carried on.

"Come and stay at my parents' house this week-end. Well, not exactly my parents. My father and his girlfriend, Wendy. You'll like them, and they'd love to have you." I was delighted to accept. It was so kind.

I felt this invitation to be a major breakthrough, and was very excited. On Friday evening Michael drove me to his parents' house, near Bath, along with Boots. The rolling countryside was beautiful, and we eventually swept up to a large, pretty house built in mellow golden stone. It had a long drive, and wonderful old front door, which now opened and out bounded three shaggy golden retrievers, barking and fussing. Then Michael's father appeared; elderly, ruddy-faced, and beaming. Extraordinary likeness to an English Bulldog I thought, and full of bonhomie. And Wendy, quieter, calmer, with warm, genuine eyes. I was welcomed like an old family friend and invited into the large, cosy kitchen and given a drink. A half-pint glass. Full of gin. A splash of tonic with ice and lemon.

"Welcome," laughed his father. "Cheers."

We had a delicious supper in the kitchen, and then retired to the lounge for more gin. It was a very comfortable lounge, a little faded and worn, a little tired, the dogs curled up by the fire. Every now and then they moved their tails, yawned and stretched. And, after a while, I found I had to turn my head, very slowly, to study a rather hideous porcelain vase on the mantelpiece.

It might have been hideous, this vase, but at least it was keeping still. If I stared at it hard. The copious quantities of gin now inside me made everything else move around the room. I was suddenly aware that the conversation was now turned on me. They were all intrigued by my appearance at 2RGJ, as the Battalion was called. They were intrigued by the fact that I was almost 30, embarking on this madcap career. I tried to assure them that I'd never seen it as a career, just an adventure, but the words were sounding rather far away this stage, and I was led to my bedroom by Nigel, Michael's Father.

Before he deposited me he asked me if I'd like tea or coffee in the morning, and which paper I preferred. I mumbled something about not being terribly sure.

Not too early, next morning, there was a gentle knock at the door, and in came Nigel looking as fresh as a daisy. He had brought me some tea, and a paper. I felt really spoiled. He slipped out of the room, and I looked around. Everything was yellow, sunny, delightfully comfortable. Out of the window the day looked bright and crisp. I could see the frost twinkling on the lawn in the morning sunlight. It was still, and very beautiful. Apparently Michael was busy today, and Nigel was going to take me into Bath and show me the highlights. Apparently the rugby club, and a nice little wine bar he knew. I should think they knew him too. He was such a character.

That day proved to be enormous fun, I enjoyed every minute of Nigel's company. He was a splendid tour guide, and knew all the interesting little nooks and crannies of Bath.

We returned home for supper, and recounted all our

adventures to the patient Wendy and to Michael. Me, getting more and more verbose as the evening went on, as the wine flowed.

"So come on, why did you join the Army Gilli?" Nigel suddenly asked. He was obviously not going to let me off the hook.

"It's a long story," I replied, not really sure how much I should tell them.

"We've got all evening," he encouraged. Michael and Wendy looked on interestedly.

"Well, let's just say that I wanted an adventure. Perhaps to escape too. Things hadn't turned out exactly as I would have wished in civvy street, and I needed a change."

"Bit of a drastic sort of change wasn't it?" Michael interjected.

"Yes, but perhaps it needed to be drastic." I struggled to find the right words. I wanted to really DO something. Something unusual. Something I'd never dreamt of before. Something worthwhile. For me."

"Was there a man involved," asked Wendy, "there usually is," she continued sympathetically.

"Well, yes, I guess there was."

Gosh, Wendy was sharp, and straight to the point. I really liked these people. Hang it! I'd be straight with them too.

"I'd had to break off a relationship that had gone on for a while, there was a lot of anguish, guilt and disappointment." I took a deep breath.

"Anguish for both of us. I couldn't see life just carrying on after that, there didn't seem enough pieces to pick up somehow. I know you can't run away from things as they really are, but a new direction and a new challenge was called for. I felt I had to do something really difficult but worth it in the end." I was rambling. It was difficult to talk about. I took another breath,

"And maybe I needed to pay a penance. To absolve the guilt. And I've paid my penance. Sandhurst was physically punishing. And now being with the Green Jackets, the only woman, not really wanted, well, that's quite mentally and emotionally punishing. I want to overcome it all."

Maybe this sounded over the top. Maybe it was. Maybe the wine had flowed too freely into my glass and down my throat. But it wasn't just the wine talking.

Nigel responded, "Life can be terribly lonely, you know," he said gently, "on your own. Especially when you get older. Don't stay alone Gilli," he said.

I smiled. And thought, "chance would be a fine thing." And aloud, "Die's probably cast now Nigel. Almost 30 you know." But I also thought a lot of other things once I was alone in my room that night. The wine had stimulated my brain. Lots of things I'd kept buried deep and jumbled up all came to the surface now. I hadn't joined the army because of a broken romance. That had been a catalyst admittedly, but I was ripe for a change really. I certainly hadn't joined the army to find romance. God I didn't want anyone to think that. I was absolutely determined that no-one could mistake me for a husband-hunter around here. Even though some of the officers, (and non-officers), and one or two in particular, were drop-dead gorgeous in every respect. I'd done this for me.

Surely that wasn't too difficult to understand was it? That whole Sandhurst episode had been something that could only be described as a star for me to reach for. For me to stretch myself to my straining limits. And for me to attain. And to glory in the attainment. It was my adventure. No-one else's. Liberating, because I struck out on my own. No-one by my side. I had had a real need to stretch. To fill a gap. OK it was a purge too, maybe. But it was something I could do on my own, not depending on anyone else, and certainly not depending upon having a "partner", a boyfriend, like so much of life seemed to when you're single. As a single girl, of 30-ish, so much felt out of bounds. I wanted to leap over those bounds. With a flourish. It was ironic that they thought I must be gay to want to join the army. Here I was among these young men and not a single woman in sight. That would have proved a good plan!

I wondered if this conversation and interest would have cropped up if I'd been a man. A man of 30 would not be considered over the hill, or odd. He would probably have been considered in his prime. This speculation, this feeling odd was just because I was an unattached female in the Army.

What was also now startlingly clear was that by joining a battalion of Green Jackets I was going to feel even more odd because not only was I made to feel I stuck out because I was single, and older than my peers, and a woman, but also my background was about as far removed from theirs as it could be.

I couldn't hide or blend into the background. I stuck out, obtrusively. How was I going to cope? I was never going to be really accepted by them. Maybe some were interested or amused, there was even some genuine affection beginning to grow, but I might as well have flown in from the planet Zog. They simply couldn't understand what I was doing there.

And yet why not? After all here were these men living a life of privilege and luxury. Beautiful surroundings, servants who lived to please, fantastic leisure facilities, stimulating company, food and drink to die for on tap, and a really worthwhile career that was exhilarating, daring, challenging, and fun too.   They wanted all this, so why wouldn't a woman?   It was just as rewarding and fulfilling for a woman..... well, it could be, if given half a chance.

My paternal grandfather, the rope splicer from North Nottinghamshire, was, by all accounts, rather a character, full of fun and practical joking.   But he was a miner, and brought home a miner's wage.   My maternal grandfather, after beginning his career as a drummer boy in the Boer War aged just thirteen, endured the horrors of the WWI trenches, and lived in the next pit village. But as his experiences in the Great War left him unable to work much again, he didn't even bring home a miner's wage.   My parents had both found work in the town, and after living in neighbouring villages actually first met at the bus stop on their way to work one morning in Nottingham.   They both worked terribly hard to give their children as much as they could and were thrilled when we made it to University.   I felt a sudden sharp pain.   What my father had really wanted was grandchildren.   He'd arranged that fabulous, no expense spared wedding, full of anticipation, full of love, with one eye on taking the grandchildren fishing and on tours of the garden.   And I had thrown it back in his face. Had he forgiven me?   Why had I had to let him down?   I loved him so much, but had it been enough?   It had been liberating to get away from all that, and to start a new life, but it did all still follow me around sometimes.

However, what had gone before made me what I was today.   But what had gone before was worlds away from all this.   As soon as I walked into The Royal Green Jackets Officers' Mess I had become confused, being the only woman in such peculiarly male surroundings, and I was also confused by their unspoken code of conduct, the "Form". No-one explained the Form. I felt awkward and rather stupid without really understanding why, or what I could do about it.

To tell the truth, I felt all of this particularly keenly whenever I had anything to do with one particular officer. He was quite a bit older than me, divorced with two teenaged children.

I had never, ever in my life come across any man who was so Gorgeous. He looked a bit like Crocodile Dundee, the same devastating, crinkly twinkle in his eye, except that he was so much more Gorgeous. Not only all that but he was charm personified.

This man was kindly, mature, intelligent, a wonderful sense of humour. He was warm, gentle, tough..... he could melt my heart at 20 paces, turn my face red, and to my intense embarrassment he could make me stutter so badly that I seemed to come out with an unintelligible language which neither of us could decipher. In short I was completely smitten. I would have walked over hot coals and bathed in them if only it could have made any difference. What was that pact I'd made with myself? But, whatever I did, this man was simply never going to see me in That Light. Not in a million years. I knew he was keen on the theatre, so I hastily organised a theatre club, with regular trips to the Theatre Royal Bath in an intimate minibus. So we could dine and, much more importantly, wine afterwards. But even after a vat full he still never saw me in That Light.

And I had to put up with the jokes that the younger subalterns constantly made about making sure they didn't sit in the shadow of my nose or they'd never be able to see the stage. This always made them hoot with laughter, and yet again I wondered how much it might cost to have plastic surgery to reduce the size of the damned thing. Would he notice me then?

Desperate for this handsome and charming officer's attention, I thought up some complicated and very obvious practical jokes to play on him. If he wouldn't fall for me and my nose perhaps he could be attracted by my entertaining ways and my fun personality. Once, on the eve of his birthday I even stayed up all night to wallpaper up his door with Happy Birthday paper in an effort to make him smile as he came out of his room on his special day. Yes, he smiled tolerantly. But That Light still bloody escaped me.

Sometimes I sat in my room, misty eyed, for hours trying to will him to knock on my door. Anytime. Day or, preferably, night. Every single encounter with this man caused me pain in my emotional wasteland. All my romantic failures in life loomed before my eyes. "What do you think you've got to offer? You're a failure remember. You're useless with men, and they wouldn't want you after what you've done. Have you forgotten anyway that this is not why you joined the Army. Can't you even be loyal to yourself."

My inner voice sneered away. And yet, like a suicide on a mission, I sought him out. Whenever I possibly could. Obviously desperate to keep torturing myself, and him, poor bloke, too. I never knew what he really thought of me, he was always so polite, such a gentleman, so smooth, unruffled, and hopefully amused. Too much to hope he was flattered. He never failed to humour me though and I always felt awkward. Too old for him – despite the fact that he was older. I felt unattractive. Far too strange an item in my unflattering combat kit and helmet with twigs hanging off it. My searing-eyeball pink lipstick flashing through the black war-paint, as though I'd forgotten to wipe my mouth after a hasty jam sandwich. I was a curiosity. We could only be colleagues, not even friends, nothing more. I knew it all along, to have been anything else would have ruined the entire episode for me. And after all, it really wasn't what I'd come for, not what I was there for. Was it?

Lonely, I spent a lot of time in my room. We finished work between 4 and 5pm, and dinner was at 8pm. That was three or four hours with little to do, and no-one to do it with. I was too proud, or lacking in confidence, to ask the other officers for some company. I often drank a bottle of wine and feasted on crisps and chocolate as I sat pondering my lonely state, trying to pluck up the courage to seek company.

The wine made me cry a lot. The crisps and chocolate made me fat. None of it comforted me, rather made me hate myself for lacking the self-control to stop doing it. That in turn lessened my chances of dealing adequately with the situation, and only increased my retreat within myself, unable to communicate or share my deep loneliness and fears.

That room became a self-inflicted torture cell where I would go and, with time dragging heavily, mull over the disasters of the day and my shortcomings. Out would come the bottle, the chocolate, the crisps, and round turned the miserable wheel once again. By 8 o'clock I'd be too full of wine and chocolate, and too full of self-pity to want to go to dinner. I did try to find some life outside the barracks. I joined the local sports club which had a decent pool. Once after a good swim I arrived back at the Mess in time for tea. Karl Theodore was there.

I struck up a conversation. "Hi Karl Theodore, I deserve some toast and honey today, I just managed 20 lengths of the pool."

"You've been swimming?" he replied, sounding a little anxious.

"Yes Karl Theodore. 20 lengths of the pool. I didn't walk it."

" Not a public pool I hope. You must never swim in a public pool."

"Why ever not?" What was wrong with the pool?

"Well, if it's a public pool the public swim there," he said, still making no sense at all. He continued, "you'll get aids. Stick to people's private pools."

"Oh stuff and nonsense you old woman," I retorted. But his attitude was very telling. We moved in different worlds, he in a world of private pools, and me in the local public one. And we each had fear of the others'.

And was he actually worried about me?

I gave up going to the sports centre sadly. There was a very odd couple who befriended me. I was more than anxious to be befriended. They played a lot of badminton, and were consequently very good. I'd never played and found I just got a very stiff neck and a very red face. I felt a bit of a gooseberry – always two against one. And then I got slightly concerned that they were after a bit of two against one off the badminton court as well, and, as they always seemed to be at the sports centre I found it difficult to avoid them there. I just stopped going.

I also tried local groups for young people. But I was, at 30, not really young enough to qualify. One such local group was for country people. They were terribly kind and sweet, but all chewed straw, or might as well have, and the chairman, Godwin Foskett seemed to be made of straw and talked of nothing but straw and which straw was best for which animal and which straw.............. I gave up.

But outwardly, I told myself, I must at all costs maintain my cheerful, sunny face. As I lay in that bed as a much-pampered guest in that lovely house of Nigel and Wendy's I managed to persuade myself that, surely, at least, I would learn a great deal from this whole episode of my life. Surely I would come out a stronger person, with more true knowledge of myself. If I could get through it there would be some sort of reward in the end. And with such positive thoughts, glorious, healing sleep at last overtook me.

The next day, was sunny again. A lovely morning. It was announced that we were all going to visit "Hugh" today. After breakfast we piled into Nigel's boneshaker, (literally tied together with string), and off we went deep into the Wiltshire countryside.

I'd no idea what to expect, but I certainly didn't expect any of what was to come. We drove down a long narrow lane, fields to either side. And then into a large clearing with a small lake, or rather a large pond. There was a mouldy, old caravan parked to one side, and someone had built a wooden porch onto the front of the caravan. Nigel stopped the car, and we all piled out. I stared at the caravan, and out came a small, elderly, white-haired man. Smiling he kissed Wendy and hugged

Nigel and Michael, then he shook me by the hand. This was Hugh.

We followed him into his caravan, and I stood amazed. It was extraordinary in there. Hugh had made all of the furniture himself, from wood he had gathered around the caravan. He'd even made the lavatory seat. I was shown it. Nigel, who'd brought two large bottles with him, was asked to make the drinks, and yet again a large tumbler was pressed into my hand. Mostly gin, but this time with a splash of vodka, and a green olive floating on top. "Cheers," we all chorused.

Then I noticed the photographs on the walls. I realised one was Elizabeth Taylor, her arm around a man. Another was Cary Grant, sitting on a horse while a man held onto the reins, yet another showed Gregory Peck.

"Ooh," I remarked. "Look! At the photographs. Are you a movie fan Hugh?" Hugh patiently explained that he was the man in the photographs. I was terribly impressed, how had he known these stars? Apparently he had been a great horseman in his time, and had lived for years in Hollywood employed by the great studios to teach the stars how to ride. He told some fascinating stories that morning as the gin flowed. We laughed a lot. Until, at last my cheeks began to numb and I couldn't smile anymore.

I looked at Nigel, his face was now scarlet. I would have sworn that I could have stuck a pin in his cheeks and he wouldn't have felt a thing. It was time to go. We all clambered aboard Nigel's chariot, waving madly to Hugh as he got smaller and smaller.

Back at the house, over Sunday lunch, thoughtfully prepared by Wendy before we'd left that morning, Hugh's life was explained to me. He'd been brought up in a wonderful stately home on a huge estate near to Bath, and had always shown extraordinary talent with horses. Eventually he'd gone to Hollywood and, charming as he was, become the darling of the stars who needed to learn to ride for their films. His parents had lost all of their money somehow, and when they died and Hugh came back to England all he could afford to keep of the estate was the plot of land where he'd parked his caravan, and the small lake which he fished for his lunch.

As Michael drove me back to the barracks that Sunday afternoon I didn't know how to thank him. I'd had the week-end of a lifetime. In fact I felt I'd lived a whole lifetime in that one week-end. It had been so fascinating, so enjoyable, so unexpected. And I felt I'd made some new, and really rather wonderful, friends.

Chapter 15 – Lots more to learn

Sometime after my week-end with Michael's parents, three new officers arrived, straight from Sandhurst. This was another major watershed because it meant I was no longer the new one around. I was interested to see that no-one in the Mess spoke much to these three officers. They were treated in much the same way that I had been. What felt terrific was that, despite coming from the "right" background themselves –

Winchester, Eton, and Rugby, they kept coming to me for advice. Wanting to know things about "the form" from me. And, even better, I found I could give them advice, tell them things that I'd discovered, and we got to be good friends, visiting each other's rooms to chat over the day's events. It wasn't the same as having girlfriends around but it was touching how some of the officers were trying more now to understand my female approach and response to things. They'd tease me, yes, but there was an element of sympathy, kindness now. From most of them.

In fact things really did change, in a most dramatic way, one lunch-time. We were all having lunch in the Mess, and Karl Theodore was at his most irritating. He had probably been rather disappointed that, thus far, he'd not managed to wind me, let alone wound me seriously, with his barbs although inwardly I dreaded them, and this seemed to drive him to ever more desperate attempts.

"How's the Assistant Adjutant today?" He asked in crisp, perfect English. The tone sneering as usual. He never referred to me by name - come to think of it neither did Robert. I drew a deep breath. Preparing myself for what I knew would come.

"Have you managed to do anything useful at all today Assistant Adjutant? Is your weapons training up to scratch yet?"

He was the Training Major as well as Company 2ic, so I suppose he did have some right to ask the question. He continued,

"Do you know how to hold a weapon yet? I've heard your nails might be too long." It was his tone more than anything. Really mean. There was no point replying so I studiously ignored him, concentrating hard on the food

138

on my plate, my appetite gone.   I felt awkward, and wondered whether to leave the room.   Then I noticed it had all gone very quiet.   One of the officers, a really decent man, George Manvers, had got to his feet. We all looked at him.   I wondered what on earth he was going to say.

"Karl Theodore," George began in stentorian tones, "I am speaking for everyone in this Mess now. We are sick to death of you trying to wind the Assistant Adjutant up. Gilli is accepted here now as one of our number. If you continue to behave so appallingly it will be you who is not accepted, not her."

It had been a short address, over in seconds. But it was played over and over in my mind as I basked in such kind and momentous words.   Had George really said that?   Was I really accepted?   All my inner fears were just that?   My own insecurities?   I was quite overcome. He'd used my name.   With such supportive intent.   My eyes filled with water.   I gazed at George at once both astonished and filled with a warm gratitude.   Murmurs of "hear hear," could be heard all around the table.   Karl Theodore sat squirming in his seat, giggling in his discomfort.

"Oh, I never meant it to harm," he blustered.

He was ignored, and the lunch continued as if nothing had happened.

The incident was never referred to again by anyone. But I felt entirely different from this point onwards.   I began to feel more a part of this close, hard-working and intelligent, inter-dependent unit. I began to feel that my contribution, however small, could be appreciated.

I did later learn that Karl Theodore, on first hearing that a woman was going to live in the Mess as a serving officer, had bet a friend that he could reduce her to tears within a week. I am delighted that he lost.

What astonished me was that, overnight, Karl Theodore became my most loyal, faithful and devoted friend. I was wary at first, but nothing was ever too much trouble for him. He clucked around me like a mother hen, protecting me and fussing around me, and I found that, underneath all that insecurity, was a genuinely kind man who really was at a bit of a loss sometimes as to how to behave. Maybe because, like me, he was a bit of a misfit. But I never did understand what he was doing as a Green Jacket. I was even more mystified to learn that he was a German aristocrat, a baron, whose father had been a famous and celebrated U-boat commander during the Second World War. Despite everything though we became firm friends. He even occasionally took me up to London, and we'd have a meal at his flat.

He'd got a long-standing girlfriend – long-standing because his father disapproved and threatened to cut him off if he got too close - who didn't seem to mind me turning up. She'd got used to sharing him with Princess Margaret on the odd occasion I learned. Apparently he was sometimes called up by an aide to make up the numbers' he said. In the end, I got terribly fond of this funny, rather lovely man.

Karl Theodore wasn't the only officer I eventually learned had aristocratic connections and a grand title. In fact I gradually found out that quite a few had. Some of them had astonishingly wonderful names, titles and estates that went back hundreds of years into medieval history. One officer's family had, until recently, owned Mont St Michael, and still did own impressive estates and a stunningly vast stately home.

But such things were never talked about. I only ever

learned of them by accident, there were certainly never any boastful references. It seemed these people didn't need to boast or show off, they didn't even need people to know of their background, position, or title. They had that charm and quiet confidence that comes with being up there at the top of the pile. They didn't need to be flashy about it. They'd have hated that. And I realised they weren't snobs either, they treated their riflemen more like friends and equals out on exercise, often referring to each other by first names or nick names. They were incredibly loyal to their riflemen, and not afraid to get close to them. Such behaviour confounded and infuriated visiting officers from other regiments. But it worked with the Green Jackets. They made it work.

I made very good friends with the Mess staff, and the Band too, both consisted of some wonderful soldiers. I'd also been introduced to the Bugle Major. The latter was a character straight out of a novel. Small, dapper, shiny smart, and with the most enormous whiskers trailing right around his head. Not long after my arrival at the Battalion Headquarters, the Colonel had asked the Bugle Major to initiate me into the mysteries of bugle calls – a most important aspect of Green Jacket life. "Reveille" was sounded outside the Officers' Mess each morning by a bugler, the Last Post was played by a bugler outside the guardroom each evening. And so on. So, one morning I went off to meet the Bugle Major in his office. It was a tiny room, just enough space for his desk and a couple of chairs. Then he called for a bugler to join us. Three people, a desk and a bugle made for a very tight fit in that very little room.

"Morning ma'am," said the good Bugle Major cheerily, "do take a seat, we are going to demonstrate some of the most common bugle calls for you." I sat down as indicated, and waited. I was obviously not expected to say anything as the Bugle Major was holding forth with an air of great importance. So I simply listened as he told me that there were bugle calls for every eventuality in life.

"Every eventuality?" I asked, astonished.

"Absolutely ma'am. Everything a rifleman could possibly want or need to do, can be translated into a bugle call," came the proud reply.

Although somewhat startled by where this line of argument might lead, I decided to refrain from asking too many questions. The Bugle Major obviously didn't like interruptions, nor did he seem to like my incredulous tone. This was serious business, but the episode did seem to be turning into a scene from "Carry On Bugle Major". Despite my urge to giggle, I tried very hard to look deferential, fascinated and grateful all at the same time. Suddenly, just as I was managing to bring myself to order, the Bugle Major turned to the poor soldier and, in a loud voice demanded,

"Sound Off Bugler!"

I stared, transfixed by the sudden awfulness of this command. Just what was the Bugler going to do?

The Bugler, confined by the limits of the tiny room, struggled to raise his bugle past limbs and furniture to his lips, before successfully blasting out several ear-splitting notes, which then seemed to reverberate around the room for several seconds.

Although my ears were ringing, my relief was, I believe, audible. "Well that's better out than in" was what I desperately wanted to say, in best Frankie Howard style, and the effort of not doing so was beginning to give me an uncontrollable fit of the giggles.

I struggled valiantly to suppress them, contorting my face into what I hoped was a look of appreciation. I didn't dare catch the Bugler's eye, let alone the Bugle Major's.

"That ma'am was the Reveille call," he informed me proudly. "Introduced in 17.. after the battle of........because........"

"Yes, lovely," I gasped. "Terribly interesting. Thank you." I was just struggling to find enough space to get up and make my escape when,

"Sound Off Bugler!" The order came once more. I jumped nervously. More violent wind-breaking followed and we were off again, not once but many, many times.

An hour of the Bugle Major demanding, "Sound Off Bugler," and then the Bugler's (to my ear all very similar) tuneless 2 or 3 notes at point blank range, followed by a lengthy explanation, was really more than flesh, blood or eardrums could stand. An awful thought struck me. Was the Bugle Major going to test me on the difference between Calls 42 and 171? Eventually I just had to blurt out my excuses.

"Excuse me Bugle Major. Sorry. Got to... got to go now. Thanks. Awfully. So very... interesting. Really...." Once out in the open, I gulped great breaths of cold air and ran to the Mess. Then I flew to my room, closed the door and, weeping with laughter, could think of nothing but what Sid James and Kenneth Williams would have made of it all.

To be honest though, I did love hearing the Buglers. There is something very poignant about their calls, something very stirring. Especially The Last Post, which could always leave me emotional. But I would always remember my initiation into their "Sounding Off".

Every Friday morning, without fail, was the Battalion Run. Every single person in the Battalion, without exception, had to complete the run. The run went out of the back gate, across several fields, and up Battlesbury Hill. If ever there was a misnomer then this was it. Battlesbury Hill was not a hill. Not when you were trying to run up it. It was a ruddy great mountain. I have to admit that, although I loved the Wiltshire countryside from my very first sight of it, and I loved being outside, I hated these Battalion Runs. I really hated them. My fitness had peaked at Sandhurst and now I simply couldn't motivate myself to keep it up. I could manage the first field all right and I just about coped with the second. It was the next field that wore me down because the "Hill" came next. Just the sight of that hill made my legs go weak.

The whole Battalion, started off together, but the crowd soon faded further and further into the distance. By the time the hill came there were, the "sickies", the Officers' Mess staff, the Band, and me.

"Here we are again ma'am," they'd all puff. The RSM, my true ally, usually managed to drive his Landrover to a spot behind a large bush at the foot of the hill. All I had to do was a sly detour round the bush, slip into the back of the vehicle and the RSM would whisk me back to the Mess in time for a quick shower and change before a hearty lunch, whilst looking impressively cool.

However, once I got to know the Mess Staff and the Band as real, endearing, cheeky riflemen who weren't in the fast lane, like I wasn't, we seemed to form a bond. A strong bond. And I began to dislike my cheating because I felt I was deserting them. So I had to start turning down the RSM's life-saving trick, and soon it became a thing of the past. Instead I ran, walked, trotted, staggered, and eventually teetered into the Mess every Friday.

I was always the last officer in to lunch. Always left, beetroot red and wheezing, to finish my plate of lunch in splendid isolation whilst the other officers drank their coffee in the ante-room and then departed to their London or country residences for the week-end. Banging their car doors, shouting at their barking dogs to "Get in". When they'd all driven off the place felt dreadfully quiet, empty. Echoing my mood. Lonely.

I didn't really have an obvious place to go at the week-end. I could go to my parents". Quite a long journey. I could play gooseberry at my sister's or one of my friends. Or I could stay alone in that great big Mess and advertise my lack of party invites and my lack of a partner. None really felt an obvious choice.

After one such lonely week-end, first thing on Monday morning, I was told by Robert that a rifleman, Rifleman Smith it was, of B Company, had joined the battalion only recently from a posting in Germany. This news didn't really interest me, until I heard what else Robert had to say. Apparently this Rifleman Smith was suspected of having committed some sort of crime out in Germany, and an investigation was in progress. There was not yet enough evidence against him, however, to bring him to trial.

"We've got to hold an identity parade," continued Robert. "You can organise that." I stared at him, I'd never been involved in an identity parade before. "You can organise that, can't you?" he asked again, impatient, giving me his hard, steely look.

"Oh yes." I recovered quickly. Not wanting to ever look inadequate in front of Robert, and really rather thrilled that he'd given me something of substance to do. "Yes, of course. I'll get onto it straight away. Er, when will it be?"

"Three members of the Special Investigations Branch, the SIB, are flying over with a witness from Berlin e specially for the parade next Monday morning. It's important. We must get it absolutely right. The parade will be held here, at Battalion HQ, just before lunch I think would be good. You'll need 8 riflemen lined up, including Rifleman Smith." I gulped, it did all sound rather important. "Sort it out then," said Robert, going back to his papers.

I'd got a whole week to arrange things. This was Big stuff. If the SIB, of whom everyone was in awe, if not terrified, were involved then this was Really Important. I knew several amenable riflemen in B Company, and started appealing to their good nature to "volunteer" for the parade.

"But ma'am," most of them complained, "what if I get picked out? What if the witness says it's me that's done it? And just what am I supposed to have done anyway?"

"No, no," I kept replying in what I hoped was a soothing tone. "You're not supposed to have done anything. No. You won't get picked out. And even if you do, well it'll all be smoothed over. No. On the contrary. It'll look good on your annual report. You know, that you've been helpful and all that." I suspected

146

this all came out a bit limply. Because I didn't really know what would happen if the wrong person got picked out. Robert hadn't volunteered any information on that score.

At last I got my 7 participants. It had taken the best part of a week, but I was all set to go by the Friday afternoon. I was rather smug about this. It hadn't been dead easy to persuade my 7 riflemen. But they were all briefed, and we were set to go. I didn't bother to discuss any of the detail with Rifleman Smith because I understood that the RSM would be in charge of all that. I just made sure that we had a room available at the appointed hour, and that my 7 chums would be there.

Monday morning arrived.

"All set for the ID parade?" asked Robert.

"Of course," I replied airily. "They'll all be downstairs in the Chief's office at noon."

"Good," continued Robert. "I've asked Rifleman Smith to come up and see me about 11.30 this morning. I think I'd better go over the procedure with him. So when he comes make yourself scarce will you."

"OK," I said. I wondered what Robert was going to say to the poor Rifleman Smith.

The morning passed slowly as usual. Then, dead on 11.30 there was a knock at the door and Rifleman Smith came in and smartly saluted. I looked up, intending to give him a sympathetic smile. My heart stopped as I stared at him horrified. I let out an audible gasp, and Robert turned to give me one of his raised-eyebrow looks. I just continued to stare, mouth open, at the rifleman.

"Is something wrong with the Assistant Adjutant?" enquired Robert icily.

"N-n- no," I managed to stutter, "no, nothing at all." And I jumped up and fled from the office.

Out in the corridor I slumped against the wall, my hands pressed to my head. I was all hot. No-one had told me. No-one had said. There must have been 2 Rifleman Smiths in B Company. This was the black one. I'd only known of the white one. I'd arranged for 7 very white soldiers to line up with him at noon. In twenty-five minutes time. How could we go ahead with an identity parade in which the only black soldier was the suspect? I rushed to the RSM's office. He would help. But he was sitting chatting, unaware of the disastrous debacle about to unfold, to the men from the Special Investigations Branch, who'd apparently already arrived all the way from Berlin especially for the parade. What on earth should I do?

"Is anything wrong?" came the RSM's voice floating after me as I ran back down the corridor.

"No," I shouted back, "everything's fine." I could only think of how desperate I was for Robert not to find out that I'd not considered this eventuality. At all costs Robert must not find out. I'd got twenty minutes. To do again what had taken me six days. My heart was thumping. I could feel my head throbbing. All jumbled up with panic.

I ran out of Battalion HQ, and in a blind panic ran over to B Company HQ. I bumped straight into their Sergeant Major. A very, very good sort of bloke.

"Whoa there ma'am!" Startled he held up his arms to stop me running straight into him. "What's the rush?"

"Oh, Sgt Major," I wheezed at him. "I need a black rifleman. And I need him now. I'm desperate. In fact, one won't be enough. I've got to have seven. Now. Have you got seven black riflemen, who could come with me? Right now?" I didn't stop to consider how this might sound.

"Seven black riflemen ma'am?" enquired the sergeant major, his forehead wrinkled as he puzzled over my request.

"Yes, now," I blurted. "I've got to have seven black riflemen. For an ID parade. To be held in 15 minutes time. They need to be there now. In Battalion HQ. The SIB are waiting. For the ID Parade, you know. Can you find some? Can you help, please………….."

"Leave it to me ma'am" he said confidently. His chest all puffed out, he strutted off importantly. To the rescue.

Deflated, exhausted, I staggered back to Battalion HQ. I went into the lavatory, and looked at myself in the mirror, hair loose, face streaked red and sweaty, I was a terrible sight. I splashed cold water onto my face and let my hands and wrists stay under the cold tap for a while. Only a few minutes and it would be noon, I hardly dared breathe.

Gathering up all my courage, I left the lavatories behind, and walked slowly to the Chief's office. I hardly dared look. Hardly dared hope as I opened the door. But there they were. Seven most excellent black riflemen, and black Rifleman Smith. The sublime Sergeant Major grinned at me.

"Thank you," I whispered at him, "there's a bottle in this for you Sgt Major. Actually, two bottles. No, seven! And share them with those seven glorious heroes!"

"Oh, thanks ma'am. I'll leave you to it then."

"Yes, carry on Sgt Major." And away he went. And, the very next second, in came Robert, the RSM and the Special Investigations Branch officers. I took a deep breath,

"I'll leave you to it then," I echoed. And bolted back to the office, to bury my head in the in-tray. Too close a shave that one. I'd been so very lucky to get clean away with it. After about half an hour Robert sauntered back.

"Go alright, did it?" I tried to keep my voice casual.

"Yes." No thanks were forthcoming, but I didn't expect any by now. I was just so relieved. A few moments went by, and then there was a knock at the door. The SIB officers came in. "We're off now, Sir," they said to Robert. "It all went very well. Thanks very much indeed for setting up the ID parade for us."

I looked up and waited, for just a fraction of a second, for Robert to introduce me and to explain I was the one who'd set it up.

"That's alright," replied Robert, completely ignoring my presence and smiling broadly. "No problem. Any time." Most gracious.

About five months into my tour with 2RGJ Robert gave me some wonderful news. He was going on a course. A residential course. In the North and for 6 weeks. I was so excited. An officer called Jonathan would be standing in for him. And he and Jonathan would begin the handover that very afternoon.

"Robert," I gasped, when he told me the news, "it's so sudden." Even he seemed pleased. He actually smiled. I did know Jonathan a little but he didn't live in the Mess, he had a beautiful little cottage in a nearby village.

Right from the start Jonathan and I got on like a house on fire. He was huge fun, and very laid back. We usually started the day with some practical joke, both of us dreaming up more and more outrageous pranks to play on each other. (Startled riflemen sent to the Adjutant's office on some errand or other often got caught in the crossfire of missiles being hurled from desk to desk.) But he was also capable and hard-working, and his black Labrador, who came to work him every day, was also very good natured. The dog was also very lazy, and just lay down to sleep through as much of the day as he was allowed.

To be honest, I could happily have forgotten my pact, again, and fallen for Jonathan.

He had something very special, and we got on so well together. We started out as friends. Then became good friends. And then, well, I started to get that little wobble in the tummy every time he smiled at me. I still didn't believe that I was "good" enough to attract one of these men. I still hadn't thrown off my self-inflicted punishment of everlasting torture to make up for cancelling that wedding. But I could have searched and found a handy way round all of that for Jonathan.

And so what happened? Well, apparently I wasn't the only one. There was this really lovely girl who lived in a village near his. She'd met him at some party, and she was smitten. Damn her. She even gave up a fantastic job so that she didn't have to travel further than Warminster any more. She apparently missed him too much if she even so much as ventured onto the motorway.

And she did a very clever thing. Although I'm sure she did it innocently, she was so nice. She didn't show any jealousy of my friendship with Jonathan. (Perhaps she just assumed I couldn't be in the running, seeing as I was some weird 30-year old in the Army). No, she befriended me too, and confided in me, and sought my advice and my help. And she was so nice, damn her, I found myself helping her, and engineering for them to have time together. It nearly killed me.

I became a sort of agony aunt trying to bring two lovely young people together. It didn't exactly give me a youthful spring in my step. But I did it. And it worked. At least they had the goodness to invite me to the wedding and it was a fantastic party. And, I could see that they really did make a lovely couple. God, I hated them. This wretched love business. I was just no good at it.

Jonathan shared the work much more evenly with me, and I was really happy. How I wished he was the real Adjutant. But eventually Robert came back, and Jonathan returned to his old role in one of the companies. The office could never be the same again. It was all gloom and sharp edges again.

It wasn't long after Robert's return that I was called in to the Colonel's office one morning.

"Well Gilli," he began, "you've been with the Battalion six months now. How are you finding things?" I didn't quite know how to answer this question. Some

152

things had been really wonderful. Great fun, satisfying. On the other hand there had been some horrible moments, intense loneliness and wretched, hopeless frustration. I'd put weight on, drank and cried alone in my room on too many lonely evenings.

"It's not all been easy Colonel," I hesitated. "But I think it's getting better. I feel more accepted now. Whereas at first I felt very out of place and I realised I was not always altogether welcome." Again I hesitated. Then I spat it out. "I really enjoyed the last six weeks."

"Yes," he said thoughtfully. And then he continued, kindly, "Our Robert is one of the best adjutants we've ever had the good fortune to have you know." Somehow I did know this, and I could quite see why the Colonel wanted to say that. I nodded, embarrassed that I'd probably said too much, and very probably got it very wrong.

The Colonel continued, "But perhaps the workload hasn't been shared very well between you." This took me by surprise. I didn't think anyone had noticed. I didn't want to moan. And I understood why the Colonel thought Robert was such a good adjutant. He was. He was a totally committed soldier who worked all around the clock. He was keen, efficient, intelligent, and hit just the right note with the riflemen. Everyone had a very high regard both for his work, and for him personally. He just didn't like having me around. My presence unsettled him. And to be fair, perhaps that wasn't his fault. I sat and waited for the excellent Colonel to continue.

"The RSM and I have been considering your role in the Battalion. We think you've settled in very well.

You've shown yourself to be capable and sensible, tactful. And you've been sensitive to the needs of the riflemen too."

"Gosh," I thought, not for the first time, "he is such a kind and decent man, this."

The Colonel continued, "we've been talking to Ralph Carter, and he is agreeable to you becoming his 2ic. That would mean you moving from Battalion HQ as Assistant Adjutant, and joining A Company as their Company 2ic. What do you think?"

Well, this was like a bolt out of the blue. I sat stunned for a moment. I didn't really know what a company 2ic would have to do, but I did realise that it would be a good move. It sounded quite important. It was a promotion. I might get responsibilities. I would get away from Robert and his gloomy office.

"Thank you Colonel," I eventually managed to reply. "Thank you very much."

So that was that. I was no longer Assistant Adjutant. I was A Company 2ic and I couldn't wait to spread the news and I popped in straight away to tell Robert.

"Yes, I know," he mumbled as he fiddled with his papers. And then he hesitated for the briefest moment and, looking up, he gave me a wide smile and added kindly "Good luck," and I felt all warm inside.

Chapter 16 – 2ic

Back at the Mess that evening everyone seemed to have heard my news, and they all congratulated me. It was as if I'd got over the probationary period, and at last, was beginning to be accepted. The younger officers from A Company all lived in the Mess, and they seemed genuinely pleased for me. One of them, Oliver Marchwood, an old Etonian from a very eminent background of very famous and hugely successful family members, was one of my favourites. He grinned at me,

"Well Gilli, I guess that makes you my boss. Hi Boss."

"Ooh I don't know about that Oliver," I quipped, "I can't see me getting you to do anything you don't want to do."

Much hilarity followed as we considered more and more outrageous things that I could and could not get the light-hearted Oliver to do. I really did feel that this was a fresh start. And I felt that getting away from the dour Robert would give me a new lease of life. Certainly Oliver was going to be great fun to work with, he had no chip on his shoulder and nor was he a career soldier. And he wasn't afraid of some ghastly girl from the coalmines of North Notts outshining him.

I already knew some of the riflemen from A company quite well. Some had been on the parachute course, and I'd also represented one or two in civilian court. After about a couple of months serving with the battalion the Colonel had asked me to take responsibility for discipline. I'd baulked a bit at this idea, wondering if it could really be appropriate, until he explained exactly what he wanted me to do. Apparently it was not uncommon for some of the riflemen to get into a bit of trouble with the civilian law – usually on a Friday evening after they'd received their week's pay and spent it at a local hostelry. Sometimes they ended up in fights or committed some petty crime. This meant they were subsequently summoned to a civilian court, and I would be expected to accompany them there – making sure they turned up – to give them a character reference, and explain any extenuating circumstances if there were any.

I'd had several such trips all over the country with various riflemen, and the experience became one of the most valuable of my army career.

I well remember one Rifleman Snozwell. He'd been involved in some petty crime when he'd gone back home to Newcastle, nothing serious really, but it could have had grave repercussions on his army career if the court so decided. The day of his court appearance we got up at 4.30am to catch the first train to London, and on to Newcastle. I got to know Rifleman Snozwell pretty well on that journey. Maybe it was because I was a woman, I don't know, but he opened up and told me all about his life back home. It was not a happy story. He was the oldest brother of five, his unemployed father drank excessively and regularly beat his mother and the boys. With no-one to care whether he went to school or not, Rifleman Snozwell had spent his days hanging around in a gang.

Eventually his father had met his end through drink, his mother continued to struggle to make ends meet, and their small house struggled to contain them all. On top of that his gang began to turn to darker crimes. Rifleman Snozwell had to choose. Did he try to keep up with his gang and hope he could help his mother, and younger brothers through a life of dealing, bullying, extortion and worse, or was there some alternative that could help him to escape this fate and still be able to send something home? After months of seamy despairing crime, of living an endless stream of lies, he ended up in the gutter of some dirty street on some desperate estate. His head was split open, his shirt soaked in blood. He gave up on life and closed his eyes. It had all been too difficult. He could no longer summon up the energy to keep trying to be responsible for his family or for himself. If he didn't wake up it would be a relief. He hated his life and what he had become.

When he did eventually wake up in hospital three days later, with his pale, painfully thin mother sobbing quietly by his bed, he had no idea how he'd got there. But he did know enough was enough, something had to change. He signed up, and had only been in the army a few months when I came across him. It didn't take much brain to see that, given the chance, and he'd had precious few of those before, this boy could make something of himself. He had veered off the track a bit, but without the army he probably stood no chance at all.

The army was his chance. A custodial sentence would put paid to all of that of course, he'd be kicked out immediately. My role was going to be crucial, and I asked Rifleman Snozwell to keep quiet for a while to give me a few moments peace to scribble down some notes that I hoped would sway the magistrates to err on the side of lenience this time. Happily the magistrates were so swayed, and we celebrated with a quick pizza before catching our train back to Warminster. Rifleman Snozwell became a model soldier after this, going on to win various adventure training awards, and rapidly being promoted. How many other boys, with little or no support at home, abused and neglected find their way into a life of bullying, crime and hopeless, helpless misery? How many of them could become Rifleman Snozwell with a bit of luck, or just a bit of help?

The first morning I reported at A Company Headquarters I tried really hard to be smart, and I even

157

tried to tone down the "Precious Puce Pink" lipstick that had become a bit of a hall mark.

I didn't feel at all confident about my new role, or how well I could fill it. It seemed rather extraordinary that someone so ill-equipped could suddenly be in such a position

Obviously not every member of A Company was glad to see me. Sergeant Major A Company, was certainly not. He made it quite obvious that, as far as he was concerned, no woman had any place in his Army, and certainly not in his Battalion, and certainly, absolutely not in his Company. He made no bones about telling everyone that he had been to the Colonel to complain about my being made Company 2ic. And I understood that he had even threatened to resign. After twenty-three years exemplary service. I was a bit put out about this, and felt uncomfortable whenever he was around. He was a very well-respected soldier, with a terrific rapport with both soldiers and officers. He was, in short, a very good man to have around. I wanted desperately to have a good rapport with him too, but he objected to me violently. I tried to butter him up but he would not be buttered. I tried to ignore him but that wasn't really practical. So, for a while I just muddled along, trying to cope with the black looks, the barbed comments.

Ralph Carter, though, welcomed me warmly. He really had the most lovely, warm, open and honest face. His smile was broad, and there was definitely a twinkle in his eye. I knew him to be another good man. Kind, decent and fair. He was married to a delightful lady, Briony, and he had four gorgeous children. That his family was the most important thing in Ralph's life was made immediately clear to anyone who met him. And I was delighted when, after being with A Company only a week he asked,

"Gilli, would you mind holding the fort for a while? I need to go out." This I took to be a real vote of confidence. After all, anything could've happened.

"No problem Ralph," I replied, suddenly feeling really important. "D'you know how long you might be?" I tried to sound as though I knew how to be in charge of a company of infantry soldiers.

"Could be quite a while actually, if you don't mind?"

"Not at all." This was really exciting. "Should I know where you are? You know, just in case."

"Good idea. The toy shop in town are having a sale this week and I must get down there to see if there are any bargains for the kids." Here was a man who had got his priorities right. The very idea of Robert in a toy shop was enough to make me snort with laughter.

Fortunately, nothing much happened whilst Ralph was away. But Oliver dropped by for a chat about some rifleman who had got into trouble with the civilian police during the week-end. His wages had apparently burned a large hole in his pocket, the pub had called loudly, the beer had tasted great, his mates had egged him on, and the policeman had looked really silly in his helmet which had just begged to be knocked off his head. One for me, it seemed. I would probably have to offer the wayward rifleman a spell in the guardhouse, and no doubt accompany him to civilian court.

Whilst we were discussing the case Ralph returned. Grinning from ear to ear, and looking very pleased with himself.

"Anything to report Gilli?" He queried.

"Well," I started, drawing in my breath, with an air of great importance, to tell Ralph my serious news hot off the press from Oliver. "It seems some poor Rifleman has got himself into a bit of a bother with...."

"Just look at this," interrupted Ralph. He opened a brightly-coloured carrier bag and produced, with a delighted flourish, a yellow plastic duck. He put it on the floor, whilst Oliver and I regarded it. Me somewhat irritated to have been interrupted.

"Look what happens when I wind it up," continued Ralph, ignoring me. Oliver grinned as we both watched the duck make its rather shaky way to the office door. I was a bit taken aback. After all I'd just been left in charge of a company of one of the most crack battalions in the British Army. The yellow plastic duck, even though it could waddle and quack at the same time, just didn't seem to do the occasion justice. However, come to think about it, no-one in A Company ever got the chance to take themselves too seriously. Ralph always shot them down before they got just enough wind to get pompous.

The Company spent its time going off on exercise on Salisbury Plain. They staged battles, playing enemy for the School of Infantry up the road, where infantry officers were trained. The trainee officers would have to pit their wits and their newly-learnt tactics against the officers and riflemen of 2RGJ. And one horrible day it was decided that I must take my place, as Company 2ic, with A Company on Exercise. I wasn't thrilled at the prospect of going on exercise with a battalion of male soldiers. I wasn't thrilled at the prospect of going on exercise full stop. But I realised that it was something I ought to do if I really wanted to be a proper 2ic. So, I agreed, and packed my rucksack full of treats, and got myself prepared to "go into the field".

I admit, I was nervous. I'd by now got used to

sharing my bathroom. And of course I was spoilt rotten with Princess Anne's lav. I did keep worrying though, what would "the arrangements" be like, out on exercise with this lot. I was also nervous about what I'd have to do, my fitness wasn't up to the standard of these red-hot infantry soldiers. And it was never going to be either. It was no use pretending. All in all, by the time the day for departure came I was feeling pretty low. However, I tried to keep my chin up, and made some silly bet with Oliver that I could keep "Precious Puce Pink" on throughout the whole event. I was all kitted up in my combat uniform, and Oliver and I helped each other to get the black war paint on. As a platoon commander he then left to check up on his men.

I wasn't too sure what my role was in all of this, no-one had said much about it, so I wandered off to Company HQ to find Ralph, and ask him how I could be useful. When I got there Ralph was nowhere to be seen. On asking the clerk I was told he'd already left for Salisbury Plain. What to do now? I wandered outside, and the only person I could see was the Sergeant Major. I decided to be brave, and behave in a professional manner. After all, I was all kitted up now and looked the part. I took a deep breath, and tried the pally approach.

"Sergeant Major, Good Morning!" I began, trying to sound enthusiastic, warm and friendly. "Where do you want me?" Perhaps not the wisest thing to ask him.

He gave me a very dark look indeed.

"Personally ma'am," he replied, positively spitting out each word, "I don't want You. Anywhere." With that he turned on his metal heel, and marched off.

Left standing there, all alone, I was completely deflated. I was at a loss as to what to do, but a pot of tea seemed like a good idea so I made my way dejectedly back to the Mess, my face still all blackened. By luck, Oliver, relaxed as always, had nipped back to the Mess for a quick cup of coffee before he got into his tank (or rather armoured personnel carrier, or APC to get the lingo right), to leave for the Plain.

"You back?" he enquired cheerfully.

"Yes, looks like it," I responded miserably.

"What happened then? You meet Old Alf? Give you a hard time did he?" Old Alf was what the Sgt Major was called by all of A Company. All except me. I somehow didn't feel myself sufficiently "in" with him to ever use his nickname, not even behind his back. Oliver, sharp as a tin tack had guessed why I had a long face.

"Yes, I met the Sgt Major," I admitted. And I told Oliver exactly what had happened.

"I'll go and sort him out," said Oliver, still cheerful.

"No don't," I pleaded, "I think it might make it worse if I make a fuss. Forget it. But thanks for listening, and thanks for your support." I was always grateful to Oliver. He was such a genuinely decent person.

He agreed not to tackle Old Alf, but did kindly suggest I join up with his corporal to go out to the Plain. And he even came out with me to the corporal's APC and ordered that room be made for me to squeeze myself and my kit into. Squeezing through the little hole at the top of the thing wasn't actually easy. Especially with half a dozen soldiers eyeing my every false move.

"Ouch ma'am, you're standing on my toe!" And "Ooph ma'am, watch where you're putting your elbow!" I didn't feel I'd made a very smooth start to my first exercise. But at least I was going to make a start, despite the odds.

I'd never been in one of these APCs before. They

were very cosy, just enough room for me, a handful of riflemen, and our kit. And the tea-making facilities. Tea-making facilities were always the essential item for any exercise. A regular "Brew Up" was the most important element in morale-building, bonding soldiers and officers together as it was something we could all do for each other. It gave comfort and warmth, an opportunity for "time out". The corporal lost no time in explaining that we would stop for our first brew up when we reached Salisbury Plain. And off we went. Rattling and bumping along in our little APC. I sat up next to the driver and his navigator, fascinated as I looked through the little glass window at the front. I was aware that one rifleman was standing up, his head through the hole, weapon in hand, at the ready. Eyeing the rather startled motorists as we sped along the road.

True to the corporal's word, once we arrived at the edge of Salisbury Plain, we stopped for a brew up. A large plastic Mess cup brimming with hot, delicious tea was handed to me. I realised I was desperate for a cuppa, and drank gratefully, draining my cup. All refreshed we set off again. This time, as we were now on rough terrain rather than a tarmac road, the little APC rolled around, bumping, lurching and juddering alarmingly. There were times when I could hardly stay in my seat. The muscles in my rear end working overtime as I was thrown from side to side, backwards and forwards. It was like being in a little boat on a great stormy sea. I was thrown around, bobbing like a little cork.

After about half an hour of this, nature began to make herself felt. And all that tea. My greatest dread. Where was I going to go? And how? I was in a small tank, surrounded by riflemen, and a whole battalion of them out there. Each bump reminded me of my plight but I knew I must try and hold on. Wait for the tank to come to a halt. I held on. Tightly. Only being able to think about one thing and it seemed like an age before the corporal ordered the driver to stop. At last, we came to an abrupt halt, and all started to wriggle our way out.

I scoured the horizon. It stretched before me, offering no hope. Never before had I given any thought at all as to why Salisbury Plain is so-called. A Plain. There are no trees on Salisbury Plain. No bushes. At least none large enough to hide a girl's modesty. I felt panic begin to grow inside me. And it wasn't the only thing growing inside me, pressing on my insides, demanding to come out. What was I to do? I'd got days of this ahead of me. Days of not drinking. But for now, I had drunk, and I needed to go. Urgently.

"Just going for a stroll corporal," I tried not to let the desperation I felt show in my voice. "Won't be long. Just need to stretch the old legs, you know awfully cramped inside there." Light, breezy tones. I set off not really knowing why I'd chosen that particular direction, there was no plan. Except to walk so far that even their binoculars wouldn't pick me out. I trudged on. And on. And on. Until the tank was hardly visible any longer. And still I trudged on. Of course they must all have realised what I was up to. This realisation only served to make me more embarrassed now. And still I trudged. The tank had long since disappeared from my view. "You can't go on forever," I told myself comfortingly. And so I got on with it. Got down to it. Pure relief. About half-way through this "process", just as I was beginning to relax into it, there was suddenly the most enormous bang. Dust and smoke flew into the air. An explosion about 100 feet away from my crouching form.

I fell to the ground.

"What the hell....?" Shocked. Dishevelled. Clothes awry. Grabbing my waistband I pulled and shoved everything together, got up and ran. All the way back to the tank. Sweating and wheezing I got there, exhausted. I struggled to catch my breath, to get my voice.

"Enjoy your stroll ma'am?" enquired the corporal smoothly, politely. There was a silence. Then the odd snort. They all turned to hide their faces. Puce faces. Eyes streaming. Their bodies shaking with laughter. Of course they'd known what I was up to. Got their binoculars out. Waited for just the right moment. And fired.

Oh dear. I was never going to take Princess Anne's lavatory for granted again.

We all piled back into the APC. Me having made a silent and solemn resolution to drink nothing more until I was safely back in the Mess - in four long days' time.

Chapter 17 – The Field Marshall

My 30th birthday was not something I looked forward to. Come to think of it, I'd been dreading it for some time. It seemed such a landmark. I'd heard too many people say "If you haven't achieved it by your 30th birthday, forget it." It wasn't just that though. It felt as if it should be a special occasion. It wasn't just an ordinary birthday, it was the Big Three-Oh, and I wanted to mark it with something special. But I couldn't do this alone, and as every other officer in the Mess was either married or had a steady girlfriend, and I was simply too proud to admit that I'd nothing planned, and to ask them if they'd mind............ So I decided to let it drift by, and hope no-one noticed what a sad specimen I was.

However, that lunch-time, as we gathered in the Mess the Colonel strode in. He had a mischievous look about him and he grinned at me. I wondered what was up. Then, in came Wolfy with bottles of chilled champagne and glasses for everyone.

"What's the occasion?" Oliver asked.

"Shall we tell them?" The Colonel asked me.

"I'd rather we didn't actually Colonel, if it's all the same to you."

"You getting married at last?" Ralph chipped in. I blushed, hot and at a loss. If they only knew how deeply that cut. I felt sick. "No, it's my birthday," I mumbled, "Cheers Colonel."

"Not just any birthday though is it Gilli?" the good Colonel continued. Thank you for that.

It's my 30th I sighed, wishing it bloody wasn't. So much for my plan.

Ralph put his arm around me. "Cheer up, you're wearing well Gilli."

"Thanks. So are you."

The champagne was lovely. I downed several glasses, and then we all had lunch together. The conversation had turned to the usual war stories, some hunting stories, their plans for the week-end.

"What are your plans for this evening Gilli?" someone asked.

"Oh, not sure yet."

"Going to be a surprise is it?"

"Mmm.." I mumbled something inaudible, and the conversation turned away. I went into some maudlin reverie. How simply wonderful it would be to have someone to surprise me. How simply wonderful it would be to have someone, surprise be damned. I spent that evening in my room, not wanting to be seen by anyone. If I kept really quiet perhaps they'd think I'd been whisked off on my surprise. And the next day, thank God the ordeal was over and done with.

Shortly after this I took two weeks leave. I was really ready to get away. More than ready. I was beginning to wonder if there was life outside of Battlesbury Barracks. It always felt very strange being away from the Army, being out of the company of soldiers. I realised that I hadn't just embarked on a new career, it was a whole way of life. Difficult to slough off. I noticed this was felt by everyone around me, and quite often when soldiers left the Army they soon wanted to come back, unable to cope in civvy street.

Some of the officers too had confided at times that they were terrified of being made redundant. Redundancy was a new evil to the Army which had hitherto provided cast iron security for life, and it cast a dark shadow over the future for those who'd never known anything other than boarding school from an early age, followed by Sandhurst, followed by life in the Mess. Such officers had a real fear of civilian life, and of working for a civilian "firm".

"I simply wouldn't know how to talk to people," one officer confided. And I realised he was voicing a genuine concern. More worrying, I realised it was true. He wouldn't know what to make of a civilian workforce, and they wouldn't know what on earth to make of him. However, a large dollop of civvy life was just what I needed right now.

A very good friend of mine, Sue, who I'd shared the house with in Balham, had recommended me to some

167

friends of hers. They were a couple with two children, aged 7 and 9. They wanted someone to look after the children while they all went on holiday for a week, on a luxury yacht, around the Greek Isles. When the couple heard that I was Sandhurst-trained they seemed to think, quite wrongly as it turned out, that I would be an ideal nanny, and hired me for the week without even meeting me. That meant that I had also not met them. But I saw it as an opportunity to bask in the Mediterranean sunshine, to play with some children, and to have a well-earned break. I had never been near a luxury yacht, and a cruise around the Greek Islands was something I'd only ever dreamed of. They paid for my return flight to Athens and a small wage on top of that. I was delighted at the arrangement. I was to make my own way to Piraeus where they and their yacht would be waiting.

The first rude shock was the couple. She, Lebanese-born and achingly beautiful, was as spoilt and as selfish as any I'd met. He was over-anxious to keep her sweet, knowing all too well, from bitter experience I could well imagine, that once she was crossed the holiday would be ruined for everyone. She took no trouble to disguise her feelings for me, and made it clear she thought I was an ugly frump who was both boring and only worth talking to as a servant. The second rude shock was the children. Two little thugs. They were simply horrible. And there I was stuck on a boat with them, in the middle of the Mediterranean.

Then I had another horrible shock when I learned what was expected of me. I was to do everything for the thugs and with the thugs. Their parents didn't want to be bothered by them at all for the whole of the week. We were to share the same yacht, but only to meet up at meal times, if the parents chose to eat on board.

Unfortunately for me, the thugs liked me as much as I liked them, and constantly ran off to join their parents. No matter how I tried to engage them and to entertain them they would scream at the top of their voices, and cry dramatically until I promised to fetch their parents to them. Once a short-fused parent arrived on the scene they would proceed to tell them how boring and useless I was. How unkind I had been. How I'd done something I shouldn't have. This endeared me to no-one. Except the crew who obviously found the whole saga fascinating and enthralling. Once or twice I got a sympathetic smile or wink, but even they were in awe of the acerbic and vitriolic tongue of the mother.

After about three days, the father, who whilst being terribly weak could also be quite sweet, blew his fuse.

"For God's sake you lot," he screamed to his family. "I've spent a small fortune on this holiday. Just to please you. To make it special for you. Just try to enjoy it. Please." I felt rather sorry for him. Although I thought him a fool. I realised, as an outsider, that he could spend all the small fortunes in the world on that family and they were never going to enjoy themselves. Never going to be satisfied. They weren't that type. He would go on, for the rest of his life, exhausting himself with the effort of walking on eggshells.

However, he managed to persuade his wife to take a slightly more flexible approach with the children, and they were allowed to be with their parents so long as I kept them entertained, and stopped them from squabbling. A task as unpleasant as it was impossible. By the end of the long and exhausting week it was only the father who could bear to say a polite, though cool, good-bye to me.

I was left, with my little bag, on the quayside of

Piraeus harbour. In the glorious golden sunshine. The sky that alluring azure blue, the water twinkling. The holiday had been a complete disaster. So far. I'd still another week before I had to be back in Warminster. There was some cash in my pocket, and a large passenger ship in the harbour about to leave for Cyprus. I'd never been there before and I'd no idea how long it would take to get there. I telephoned the airline from a little call box, and postponed my flight for five days. I purchased the cheapest return ticket available for Cyprus, and got on to the ship.

The cheapest ticket was a "deck ticket". This meant that I had the use of a deckchair whilst on board. This sounded rather good, until I realised that what it meant was that I only had the use of a deckchair whilst on board. Once I found out that the journey to Cyprus would take two nights, I had to accept that I had to spend two nights out on deck under the chilly sky in said deckchair to get there, and then follow that immediately with two nights back. There'd be little, or no, opportunity to look around. However, I was not daunted. I was free. Free to do as I pleased, within the confines of one deckchair, and the ship. I had meal tickets, tickets for the entertainment on board each evening, my books and my Bruce Springsteen tapes, the sun shone, the sea was calm and very beautiful. As long as the weather held, what more could a girl, free and single, possibly have wanted? So I took up residence in my deckchair, and prepared to relax. And it wasn't an unpleasant experience at all. I met some wonderful young Polish tourists, who adored me for my Bruce Springsteen tapes and the week sped by in a haze of laziness.

On my return to barracks, tanned and relaxed, the

Officers" Mess was in full swing preparing for an important Mess night. Several VIP Green Jacket guests were invited, and to cap the lot Field Marshall Lord Edwin Bramall was to be guest of honour.

"Is he a Green Jacket then?" I asked Oliver.

"About the most important," he replied obviously horrified at my ignorance.

The Mess staff were definitely preoccupied; when Corporal Smith brought in my early morning cup of tea every morning that week there was always sugar in it.

"Oh Smithy," I said groggily each morning, "I hate sugar in it you know."

"Sorry ma'am, won't happen again." But it did, every morning that week.

We were all getting a bit on edge. The band had been practising the pieces they would play following the dinner for weeks. The silver was all getting an extra polish. Wolfy was snapping everyone's heads off. I was quite calm. After all, I wouldn't have to do anything. So long as I didn't drink too much liquid at the table I'd be alright. (We could never leave the table until the guest of honour left, not even if we were desperate. Sometimes the guest of honour lingered too long over the port after a six-course meal that had taken hours to get through, and the waiting was agony. So much so that sometimes one looked at the empty decanters and wondered if they could be slipped under the tablecloth for an alternative use. As usual, much easier for the chaps).

Then, the morning of the great dinner, the table plan went up in the hall of the Mess.

"Gilli, have you seen?" gasped Oliver as he came rushing into the anteroom.

"Seen what," I replied looking up from my

newspaper.

"The table plan. For this evening."

"What about the table plan?"

"You're next to „Dwin Bramall."

"Nice one Oliver, not falling for that," I returned to the paper.

Oliver, unperturbed, continued, "Wonder why they've put you next to him. I mean, well, you know......" he ended limply.

George came into the Mess then. "Wow, Gilli. What have you done to deserve this high honour? Sitting next to Lord Bramall eh?" This did catch my attention, and I got up to have a look at the plan for myself. There I was between Lord Bramall and Karl Theodore. Apparently Karl Theodore had been Bramall's ADC and they still kept in touch. I rushed back into the anteroom, alarmed.

"Oh God, what's he like this Lord Bramall?"

"Believe me now do you?" Oliver beamed. And then everyone joined in. Telling me how the Field Marshall sternly disapproved of women in the army, how he wouldn't talk to me. How he never talked to subalterns, and certainly would stonewall me, a rank outsider. I began to dread the dinner. I wondered, for a mad moment, if I could feign illness or break a leg falling down the stairs. I'd probably be made to turn up if I broke both legs.

I made huge efforts on that important evening to look all right. It wasn't just a feminine thing, I'm sure everyone made that effort. I just didn't want to let anyone down, least of all myself. The Mess staff had certainly worked like stink ensuring every last detail was correct. And the dining room did look astonishingly grand and beautiful. But in my mind I had only one question, "What on earth was this man going to be like?" If he did refuse to talk to me how should I behave? I felt rather indignant to think I might be ignored, but nervous of how I might react if I was angry. All this confusion, anticipation and emotion was exhausting. I was worn out before the evening even began.

Full of dread as I descended the stairs, I would have given anything at that moment just to have a sandwich in my little room. Safely away from all this fear of the unknown. Actually I didn't have the appetite for even a sandwich.

We all gathered, somewhat self-consciously, in the Mess, at 7.30pm. With drinks in our hands we were all very aware of the white-haired, stocky man chatting with the Colonel. There were obvious hallmarks of nervous politeness about the officers who were honoured with his attention. There was forced laughter and a bit of bowing and scraping. And then, I could see the Colonel advancing on me. I tried to look away and disappear into a wall. It was no good, he seemed intent on seeking me out.

"Come and meet the Field Marshall Gilli," he ordered in his charming and friendly way, and he held out his arm supportively and scooped me up and steered me over to the Great Man.

"No, Colonel, I'd like to just stay with you please," I silently pleaded. My heart was sinking, my knees weakened. I still had no idea what I could possibly say to him.

Of course, I need never have feared. He turned out to be absolutely charming, a most entertaining dinner partner, and he was interested in everything I had to say. I had a thoroughly good and happy time. I was really proud to have had the opportunity to meet such a great man at such close quarters.

The dinner night was a huge success. And Lord Bramall, bless him, didn't linger over the port.

Chapter 18 - Matchmaking

Shortly after the success of the dinner night the battalion was to stage a Fire Power Demonstration in Battlesbury Bowl. This was an opportunity for the British Army, with the support of the RAF, to demonstrate the country's formidable military firepower, and to impress foreign dignitaries with the weapons which were for sale. A shop window with a difference. HRH Prince Andrew was to attend the demonstration, and I, as A Company 2ic was expected to take part.

I paraded with the rest of the company outside company headquarters at 7 o'clock that morning. The Sgt. Major gave us our orders, Ralph gave us a pep talk, and off we went, jamming ourselves into armoured personnel carriers in full combat kit and war paint. The APCs rattled their way down to Salisbury Plain in full view of the Bowl. We had to wait now, for a couple of hours, whilst all the dignitaries arrived and took their places.

Eventually we received the order to begin the demonstration, and to my surprise all of the riflemen leapt out of the APC and ran off into the distance, expecting me to follow. In full combat kit I confess I just couldn't keep up with them. I could hear their shouts and screams, as they pretended to do battle, getting fainter and fainter, while I huffed and puffed my way through the undergrowth. I could just make out that they were on their way to other APCs in the far distance waiting to collect them as they made a getaway. But I was far too slow, and to be fair they'd had lots of practice and all the required training, whereas I'd had none. That morning had been the first time I'd even been aware of the plan. Looking back I can see clearly that, although I was grateful to have been included, this was not an all-out effort on the part of the Army to integrate a woman into a hitherto male world. I just simply didn't receive the same training or briefing as the men. That was to come later - for the next generation of females. This was more the sowing of a seed, part of a first attempt to start changing things for women. I was a part of an experiment, an inkling of things that might come about if considered desirable and worthwhile. And this particular inkling was finding the going rather tough.

My legs were beginning to buckle, the sweat was dripping down, and my chest was heaving and wheezing. I was not as fit as I had been at Sandhurst, I'd lost some of that motivation and had slowly sunk back into my bad old ways. Undoubtedly some of my female friends I'd trained with would have tackled this more competently. They'd have worked at the fitness with more relish than I had. Out of the corner of my eye I spied a small bush. Small yes, but just large enough. Hoping that HRH Prince Andrew and the dignitaries, let alone the Adjutant, were not looking, I ducked behind it and flopped down. My plan was to hide there until everything was over and then walk back, several miles, to the Mess. The relief I felt in my back and shoulders as I allowed my backpack to slide to the ground with a satisfying thump, was wonderful. Then, as I was just beginning to relax, I noticed a droning noise in the distance which, as I listened, got louder, nearer. I looked up and just caught sight of a Harrier jet skidding across the sky, and then "Bang!" The bowl reverberated as the jet released its cargo onto the target. Not too close, but close enough.

My mouth went dry as my heart pounded with the shocking realisation. I had realised my dilemma. To move and make a run for it would make me a laughing stock to the whole arena, might even mean the demonstration had to be interrupted whilst I was escorted to safety. Big Trouble lay that way. But to stay might mean Big Death.

I thought of Robert's face if he ever had the satisfaction of knowing what had happened, and decided to stick it out. I had a great ring-side view of the British Army's firepower in all its glory, and I can honestly say it was terribly impressive. Awesome and terrifying. I shall never forget it. For about an hour I stayed in that hiding place, listening to the commentary being given by our Training Officer in calm and cheerful tones and bracing myself, eyes tight shut, for each cataclysmic explosion, each mammoth reverberation. Watching with awed fascination as great showers of earth shot high into the sky.

At last, I gathered that the show was at an end, and the VIPs were led away. In relief and earnest gratefulness for my life, I continued to lie there, enjoying the peace that had been restored to the Bowl, wondering if anyone had missed me. They'd probably realised I'd figured a way out of things. Probably thought I'd wandered off to enjoy the view of the other side of the hill and gather spring flowers for my room. Like girls do. I got all my kit together, shouldered it, and staggered off in the general direction of the Mess. I realised that I would need to clean myself up before anyone caught sight of me. And after that an ice-cold gin was calling to me. Just so long as no-one found out I'd nearly wrecked single-handedly one of the most important events in the Demonstration Battalion's calendar.

A few weeks later, we were all looking forward to a large party that had been planned to celebrate the anniversary of some battle that had been fought and gloriously won during the Boer War. I'd invited some of my Sandhurst friends to come, and I was pleased Tina, and her boyfriend Tony, and Jemima had accepted. Usually my friends weren't of much interest to anyone in the Mess, but I was curious to see how these red-blooded males might respond to Jemima. I had never met a man who didn't at least stare longingly at her, she was so gorgeous to look at, and such a lovely person.

My room in the Mess was next door to the room of Jamie McCall-Browne. He was a Captain, about Jemima's age. His father, a Brigadier, had been a Green Jacket before him – as was so often the case – and had been captured by the Germans in the Second World War and held prisoner in Colditz Castle. Apparently the experience had been so devastating for the poor man that he could now not bear to talk about it. Jamie was an exceptionally gentle soul, a Catholic who had been to school at Ampleforth and continued to be deeply religious. I suppose he was also quite old-fashioned in his attitude, in particular towards women.

To Jamie a woman was to be cherished, protected, treated with kid gloves, and was definitely not to be tampered with until married. As I led Jemima to my room that evening before the party, Jamie was just emerging from his room heading for the bathroom.

"Jamie," I said, "this is my good friend Jemima. She's come for our party. We were at Sandhurst together."

Jemima held out her hand, and I watched his response. He just stood there and stared at her for a full minute, and then, remembering himself, he smiled taking her hand gently in his,

."...er hello. Jemima did you say? It's a pleasure." As I opened my door for Jemima I looked back at Jamie still standing in the corridor. He shot me a look of pure entreaty. He was smitten.

We all had a great night. These guys really knew how to throw a party, the champagne flowed, the band played into the early hours. We had dodgems and a merry go round and it was great to see my friends again, and to share with them some of the more awful scrapes I'd got into recently. We hooted with laughter at all sorts of things I had never been able to find funny before, and eventually, in the early hours, we went off exhausted to sleep.

Jemima, Tina and Tony all left the next morning, and I felt suddenly lonely again. It was a Sunday, I felt jaded and had no plans. Just before lunch, as I was still putting myself together, there was a soft knock at the door. It had to be Jamie.

"Has Jemima gone?" He enquired.

"Yes, she's with the Cavalry you know. She's their Assistant Adjutant and had to get back for some important drinks party in London. Sit down Jamie. Are you alright?"

"How long have you known her, Jemima?" He said the name with great feeling. I told him all about our friendship at Sandhurst. How she was a great

178

personality, a real character. "Will you invite her again, do you think?" he almost begged. "Could you, soon?"

I promised to invite Jemima to a black tie dinner a couple of weeks later, and then spent hours with Jamie most evenings in my room, him asking endless questions about Jemima, his eyes misting over.   When they met at the dinner I was delighted to see that she responded to his charm, and they became a bit of an item.

However, I had my misgivings. Jemima was a woman of the very real world, she liked a drink or six, and a laugh or fourteen, and I wasn't at all sure how she would cope with being protected by Jamie, treated as delicate china with kid gloves, awaiting consummation only in married bliss.   She did very well at first, and enjoyed the novelty, but sadly it soon wore off. Jamie was heartbroken, and I found it hard not to feel I'd let him down.

The whole episode had been interesting to me though. The Green Jacket officers were a specific breed in their general approach to women.   They had been appalled, but fascinated, by the fact that I, a woman, had joined the Army.   And for this reason alone wouldn't have dreamt of considering me as a "partner". Jemima, with her exceptional beauty, had broken through this barrier. However, had their relationship been successful Jamie would have insisted she gave up her career.   (As it happens Jemima would have been only too happy to comply, she had no plans to work for any longer than she had to, and refused to take anything too seriously until then.)   Why didn't the Green Jacket officers like their wives to work I wondered? Was it because they might be more successful than them?   Robert obviously couldn't cope with any competition from a woman in the office.   Maybe it was a highly developed sense of responsibility and duty that led them to believe that they must support their wife to keep their honour? Indeed, when George proposed to his high-powered and capable girlfriend he had insisted that she give up a highly paid and senior job at a stock brokers in the city before they wed. Apparently, she complied without a murmur.

Was this perhaps an upper class trait? The Green Jacket officers were certainly all unmistakably upper class with their confidence, charm and code of behaviour.

Interestingly, it wasn't just money that made them upper class, although I gathered that they were all independently wealthy despite the fact that this was never mentioned. These men were all educated at the best, and most expensive and exclusive public schools in England, as had their fathers and their fathers' fathers. Was their upper class-ness something inbred through generations then? Their being in the Green Jackets often seemed something of a family tradition too going way back.

And I, where did I fit in? I had become a little confused. I was from a working class background, and yet I had gone to the most exclusive military training academy in the world, rubbed shoulders with the elite, and now lived in an exclusive and upper crust environment, surrounded by representatives of the aristocracy and upper classes. I didn't really fit in here, and I didn't fit in back there. I had some adapting to do which needed sensitivity, humility and wisdom in doses which were, in reality, beyond my means.

Chapter 19 – Camel on parade

During one early morning "O (orders) group" in company headquarters one day, Ralph explained that we were to have a Battalion Muster Parade the following month. The Colonel; Regimental 2ic, and all the Company Commanders would be expected to be mounted. So we had to find Ralph a horse. This caused some amusement as Ralph was not a keen horseman. He didn't know one end from the other. But Ralph himself had other ideas. After the "O group", once everyone had gone off to get on with the day's business, he called me into his office, and closed the door.

"I've had an idea. A Great idea," Ralph confided. He sounded very excited. "This muster parade, next month. You know how the company commanders are expected to be mounted?"

"Yes," I replied, "go on."

"Well, the Colonel didn't say on what." I looked blank. "I'm not going to ride a horse," explained Ralph.

"Why not?"

"Because I'm going to ride a camel," he said triumphantly.

Apparently, he'd dreamt up this mad idea as soon as he'd heard about the mounted parade. No-one was to know about it, apart from me. He'd looked at a local map and discovered that we weren't that far from Longleat. Longleat had camels. He was going to telephone them and ask to borrow one for the morning.

"Oh yes. Just like that?" I put my spoke in. "Really."

"Oh come on," begged Ralph. "Do say you'll help. It'd be fantastic. Such a scream to turn up on parade on a camel. We won't let anyone else into the secret. Promise you'll keep mum."

I could see that it would be a huge laugh if we could pull it off. And thinking about it I was sure we wouldn't get into much trouble. After all, the Colonel was such a good sport I was quite sure he'd see the funny side to it. So the idea did have its appeal......

"OK," I agreed. "Let's phone Longleat this morning. Just to make sure that we really can borrow a live camel."

So later, when all was quiet, Ralph called Longleat. Afterwards he came rushing through to my office, closing the door behind him.

"We're on," he said excitedly. He was dancing round the room. Grinning from ear to ear. "This is going to be great!" He explained that we had been invited to Longleat the following week. They had just the right sort of camel apparently - a ten-year old female called Ivy who was used to crowds, as she often gave rides to the visitors at the park. Apparently good natured too. Oh good. So, we looked forward to meeting Ivy, and getting to know her prior to the parade.

The following week, as per the invitation, Ralph and I had a wonderful secret morning at Longleat getting to know Ivy, and finding out all her little foibles from her keeper. She really was a wonderful character, and thankfully very biddable. Ralph was beside himself with excitement. All the arrangements were planned. Ivy would be delivered to the barracks in a special trailer early on the morning of the parade. Her keeper would come with her, and fit her with a halter, with a long rope. Just as the parade was about to get started I would lead

Ivy out of the trailer, Ralph would mount her, and I would then lead the both of them onto the parade ground. To the stunned amazement of officers and riflemen alike. We wriggled with excitement when we secretly imagined what it would be like. Goodness only knows what Ralph was like as a child waiting for Christmas. He certainly could hardly bear waiting for the day of the Muster Parade.

And really neither could I. Robert, as Adjutant, was being dreadfully pompous about making all the arrangements, and every time he rang to check that A Company was getting properly prepared I was almost beside myself with glee. Ralph and I would huddle secretly in his office, to go over our plan. Like 2 small children planning a raid on the sweetie shop.

At last the day dawned. I was up with the lark, and rushed over to A Company Headquarters. Ralph had been there practically all night so excited he couldn't sleep, and preferring to wait at the scene of the crime-to-be-committed rather than in his bed.

"All set Gilli?" he asked unnecessarily.

"All set," I replied. And then we saw the large trailer draw up at the guardroom. The guard knew nothing of the contents, but Ralph had ordered them to let it straight through and direct it around to us. We went outside to await their arrival. The keeper greeted us and we three conspirators went inside the large box to say good morning to Ivy. She seemed perfectly calm and rather aloof from our excited exchanges. But she did smell. Strongly actually. I had to hold my nose. I kept wondering if it might be worth popping quickly to the stores to grab a gas mask.

Ralph kept asking me to go and check what was happening on the parade square.

"Nothing much yet," I reported. Then, next time, "a bit more activity now." Then, "yes, everyone's beginning to line up." At last, it was time to get Ivy out of her box. I dusted myself down, and put on my cap. Hoping I was smart enough in my "Number Twos". I helped Ivy out, leading her by the rope. Ralph, with some difficulty, mounted her, and with much giggling, and great anticipation I led Ivy towards the parade square. As we approached the square I suddenly saw a scene of great chaos. Instead of the ordered smartness of lines of officers and soldiers ready for inspection, I saw horses bolting in every direction. Their riders struggling and failing to keep control. Robert's horse was galloping at top speed towards the fields below Battlesbury Hill. Robert, now hatless and looking totally astonished, was screaming something inaudible as he disappeared from view. A most unusual, and an almost unbearably satisfying, sight. By now all the soldiers were rendered helpless with astonishment and laughter. Ivy continued to follow my lead, seemingly an old hand on the parade square, and rather proud, as if she was above all of this nonsense. None of the mounted officers were to be seen anywhere. Only the Colonel had managed to recover both himself and his horse. He was still bravely attempting to take the parade, and although his horse refused to face the camel, so that the Colonel had to turn right round in his saddle, and we just saw his head above his horse's hind quarters, he still managed to return Ralph's smart salute as we "marched" past him.

As I led Ivy off the parade square and back towards her box I was aware that we had rendered the Muster Parade a complete shambles. Everyone remaining was dismissed, although it took some time for the square to empty.   Everyone loudly discussing the morning's antics.   Lots of "did you see..........?" And "what about............?" Some of the soldiers rushed round to A Company to get a closer look at Ivy.   Apparently Robert's horse had still not returned him to the barracks. Goodness knows where they'd got to. We should have been concerned, but we were far too wrapped up in all the attention.   It was only now that Ivy's keeper gave us some rather vital information.

"Camels have a very strong and very distinctive smell you know," he said to his captive audience. I had noticed that actually.   And then he added, "horses are absolutely terrified by it."

Ralph and I looked at each other. So that's what had happened. "Ooops."   We hadn't planned for that.   But then we both agreed that even if we had known we would still have gone ahead. Seeing Robert like that was definitely worth facing the inevitable music.   And there were a few well-chosen words from several quarters to be faced before the day was out, which we just had to face stoically. Although it was a bit difficult to look too shame-faced.   It had, after all, been so worth it.

This wasn't the only parade made memorable for being somewhat out of the ordinary.
The first year I was with 2RGJ was a year when they were responsible for the Horse Guards Parade. This was a large and important event to be held in Horse Guards Parade, just off Whitehall in London. HM The Queen Mother would be taking the salute, and a reception would be held afterwards at the Mansion House. I was very much involved in the preparations, the organisation, and I was excited. However, as I was so keen on drill, and marching with band, horses, and ceremony, I was disappointed not to be allowed to actually take part. The

Green Jackets are famous for their distinctive marching. They march in double quick time, and they actually look as if they are trotting. I, as a WRAC, (Women's Royal Army Corps), officer would have looked a bit out of place, I admit. In the end I was happy just to be there, to share the occasion, proud of our riflemen. As I watched the ceremony I recognised, not for the first time, that the British Army do this better than anyone else in the world. There's some real split-second timing going on in some of the routines. Accuracy is all as those soldiers, and horses strut their stuff to the stirring music. But you can trust that every single one of them won't have a hair out of place. And every single soldier, every horse, every single piece of kit, will be polished to shining. Moving as one. So much effort, so much commitment, and achievement, so much to be proud of.

Just prior to our going up to London for this event the Colonel had called me in to ask me to do something special. He knew how I felt about not having an active part in the occasion.

"Gilli, I know you are a bit disappointed not to be marching. But we are so proud to have you with us. And to make up for your disappointment we have an important job for you to do on this outing."

"Oh really, Colonel? Thank you. Er, what's that?" I was excited and curious. What could it be?

"You realise that the Queen Mother will be taking the salute, and that a reception will be held for her, in the Mansion House afterwards?"

"Yes," I replied holding my breath in anticipation.

"Well, we'd like you to be in charge of her lavatory."

"Pardon."

"The Queen Mother's lavatory. We'd like you to take responsibility for everything being, well, you know, ship shape."

"Oh. Ship shape. The lavatory. I see. I think."

"No doubt everything will be explained to you by one of her aides. It'll all come together, don't worry."

So I went away musing about HM's lavatory all coming together, until we went up to London.   And indeed one of her aides did look me out – not really difficult to spot me in that crowd I suppose – and explained that a special lavatory would be delivered and a special room would be fitted out with all of Her Majesty's special kit, as it were. My role was to nip in there beforehand to check that everything looked in order. Fit for a queen.

And indeed I did. And indeed it did.

I thought of my lav back at the Mess.   And its connection with Princess Anne. And I mused. The only relations I had with royalty, tenuous as they were, were through their lavatories. Shame that.

Chapter 20 – Nothing lasts forever

As the months wore on, I was given more and more responsibility. I found myself attending civilian court quite regularly with the riflemen who'd got themselves into trouble with the civilian authorities. I also found myself running the firing ranges for training. With live ammunition. This was probably my most demanding responsibility. I was grateful to the Colonel, and to Ralph, for showing such confidence in me, but I was even more grateful to the riflemen for their confidence. I also continued to go out on exercise, and felt that I'd achieved the pinnacle of success when, out on Salisbury Plain one morning, the Sgt Major woke me up with a cup of tea, and a cheery, "Good morning ma'am, nice cuppa for you. You did well yesterday, by the way." And that was it. Firm friends ever after. I couldn't actually recall what I could possibly have done well, but whatever it was I was glad of it. The Sgt Major was a friend worth having, and I very soon discovered what an excellent person lay beneath that hitherto prickly façade. Exercises weren't so daunting now I wasn't loathed. I nearly enjoyed them.

During the long, warm lovely summer months I decided to hoist my colours to the cricket team, under the exuberant captaincy of Oliver. Each of their matches was a story of its own, Oliver flamboyant with his innate talent. And 2RGJ won the Army Cup that year.

It was wonderful to be able to be part of that great cause for celebration. We felt on top of the world.

Then, soon afterwards, one awful day, the world stopped.

I had the most terrible news. If I had had the chance to ever speak of the news that would cause me the most pain and anguish to hear then this was it. Those awful words when spoken could never be unspoken however much I wished it. The words were said kindly and gently by the padre who had waited anxiously in the Officers" Mess all day for my return from duties. I realised with a small stab of fear, because it was the padre and his face was taut and pale, that I was about to be told something very personal, very grave. He gently led me, legs weak with dread of the unknown, out into the privacy of the fresh air and said,

"Gilli, I am very sorry to tell you. Your father died of a heart attack this morning."

Just that. Straight to the awful point. I knew it must be true. No-one would say such a terrible thing if it weren't. The world stopped. Everything was silent. Nothing moved.

My senses numbed. After a while some of my faculties returned. I realised how rotten it must have been for the padre to have to wait around to tell me something so horrible. I thanked him and began to stumble off. Just wanting to be alone. Wanting to sob, and sob, and sob. Dead. So that's it then. Dead. No more. Gone. Never coming back.

After what must have been a decent interval the padre came into my room. Did I want the MO? Could he fetch me anything, anyone? "Actually padre I just want my father" didn't seem an appropriate thing to say. Apparently my mother was being looked after by friends, and my sister had gone to her. They were both very anxious to speak to me as soon as possible. Would he like me to dial the number from the phone on my desk? Apparently as my father had already died I couldn't get compassionate leave. He had to still be alive for that. "Oh God, Daddy."

Everyone was terribly, terribly kind. And I was given a rail warrant to get up to Nottinghamshire the next day. Once there my mother, sister and I became aware that we had simply the best friends in the world. My father had been a hugely popular person and everyone was shocked and deeply saddened by his death so suddenly at 62. We were surrounded by love and care and friendship, and my God did that help. Letters flowed in and we wept over them for long hours. We drank our way through my father's stock of whisky and smoked our last cigarettes. It was a last thing we could do for him. He hated us smoking, and we'd all agreed that, for him, we'd stop after the funeral.

I suppose experience of death does distort behaviour in all sorts of ways and I found that I couldn't sleep in my bed at night. I had to sleep in the kitchen wrapped in one of my father's huge, he was six foot five, woolly jumpers. It felt and smelled like him, and at night that was the only place I wanted to be. I talked to him still, and felt very close to him. I remembered the, very happy, times we'd had of late. He'd loved visiting me at the Officers' Mess where everyone had made a big fuss of him. Thank you. I had made him proud. The Passing Out Parade at Sandhurst had thrilled him. Everyone kept telling me how proud he'd been of my recent achievements. Thank you. There were still many things I wanted desperately to say to him, so much I wanted to tell him. He'd been snatched away long before I was ready. But I knew he knew I loved him, always. And I knew he loved me. It was all that really mattered in the end. And it was enough.

So many people wanted to come to the funeral that we were advised to change the venue from the ancient village church where my father had loved being a churchwarden and lay reader in recent years, to a larger church in the nearby town. My mother, sister and I, defiant against the tears, had been given "magic pills" by a quite redoubtable 84-year old friend, Edna. So determined was she that we were going to get through the day with dignity and be a credit to our dear departed. And indeed she arrived at our little cottage at 8 in the morning to make sure we had breakfast.

"Now," she said to us as she swept through our back door and spotted us pale and limply hanging around the kitchen, "You are going to have breakfast aren't you." An order. "You remember the donkey don't you? They'd just got him used to not eating when he died." We smiled weakly and helped her to find the plates. She'd had the foresight to bring the bread for toast. She'd also brought jam, marmalade, butter, tea, coffee, milk and honey. Bless her. She knew we'd been on a diet of whisky and cigarettes to deaden our raw emotions. The day I had arrived home my sister had, thankfully, taken charge of the cooking. At tea time she told me, "The pizza's in the oven." Three days later she told me, "Oh, the pizza's still in the oven."

While Edna fussed over getting some breakfast into us she kept on chatting, chivvying us on and, funerals on her mind, she started to tell us about her brother Bert's sad demise.

"Well, while we were out shopping yesterday I thought about Bert," she announced buttering yet more unwanted toast, "and remembered when he died last year... all of a sudden when he'd only popped round for a spot of lunch." (Note not to pop round there for a spot of lunch.) "Walter and I were in such a state we never thought to eat our lunch. We went all to bits. I remember we just got straight in the car to go and tell our Jean, (their daughter who lived a good couple of hours drive away.) When we got to our Jean's and told her I suddenly realised that we'd just left Bert where he was, and asked Walter if he thought he'd be alright on his own, and he said "Oh yes, we left him propped up against the kitchen table so he can't move until we get back."

My sister, mother and I looked at each other. At least she'd got us smiling. Edna was a gem. And there were more gems, said kindly to cheer us up. Mary Bagshaw, the ancient, and blind, church organist and local farmer's wife also wanted to reminisce on this seemingly favourite topic,

"You know, when my old mother died it was all over before I knew about it, and I couldn't go to the funeral. My husband Arthur said, „Mary, I'm sorry, I've just remembered your mum died and I forgot to tell you'."

Harry Stacey, a close neighbour of my parents, declared loudly,

"If only that bloody cockerel of yours could have kicked „is bucket instead of ye father." We actually loved our cockerel's early morning call, but the idea of swapping him for my father was appreciated, and we nodded our heads vigorously in full agreement.

My aunt, determined that my mother's life should return to some normality and the gap my father had left be filled as soon as possible, counselled "…. and you must get a dog now Joan."   Honestly, what people say at these times. But it was all somehow very comforting. People cared.

The funeral was very uplifting.   I was quite sure my father enjoyed it.   So well-attended.   Such wonderful, and true, things were said about him. I felt we'd all done him proud.   Just as he deserved.   He was special.   I would miss him, achingly. But I also knew I would still carry him around with me in my heart, still try to please him. Still continue trying to make him proud.

Our final farewells done, it was time for me to return to barracks. I was a bit fragile, vulnerable, weepy and my sadness felt like a heavy lump. But I didn't want to let anyone down, least of all my father.   He would have wanted me to get on with my job and "get stuck in". So I tried my absolute best to do just that.

And then, without my having the slightest idea, my time was up.   My first posting drawing to a close.   I received a letter from the WRAC Command informing me of my next posting. I felt ill. How could I possibly leave? 2RGJ had become something that I belonged to. I'd never had such a feeling of belonging before.   It was so strong.   So special, I treasured it, never wanting it to break.   And yet, I wasn't even sure just when I'd begun to feel I belonged. Hot tears stung my cheeks. I loved being here. Loved being with them and I loved them all. Every single one of them.   I wanted to be with them, forever.   Yes, I could remember a time when I hadn't felt that way.   But things had changed, slowly.   Very slowly, but very surely. I sat in my room, stunned at the change that faced me. Staring out of the window at those peaceful, calm fields. Not wanting to disturb anything. Not wanting to face facts.

I went to see the Colonel. To explain about my posting but of course he knew all about it already.

"Well Gilli, you've got a choice," he said.

"Have I Colonel?" I hadn't realised.

"Yes, you can accept the posting you've been given. Or, you could stay with us."

"Stay with you?" I was thrilled at the prospect. I wanted to stay more than anything.

"Yes. However, you need to take time to think about it. 2RGJ is being posted too. To Dover. From there we are doing another Northern Ireland stint. We'd be very happy for you to remain with 2RGJ, and to join us in Dover. But you wouldn't be going to Northern Ireland with the rest of the battalion. You'd stay, probably as Assistant Adjutant again, in Dover. It would be very quiet, not many of us around."

I thanked the Colonel. Profusely. I regarded it as a high honour to be invited to stay with 2RGJ. And it was what I wanted. I skipped back to the Mess. There I bumped into "Wolfy", and Corporal Black.

"Wolfy, Wolfy," I cried, "and Corporal Black. The Colonel has said I can stay with you. Stay with 2RGJ. I'm so thrilled."

"Well that's great," they agreed. Wolfy continued, "You do know ma'am, don't you, that we are being posted too? To Dover? And then we'll be taking it in turns to do tours in Northern Ireland?"

"Yes, yes" I replied, not wanting to be bothered with the details, "the Colonel told me all that."

"Might be a bit boring for you ma'am," he suggested bravely. "Staying back in the office in Dover. What's your alternative posting?"

"Cyprus," I replied.

"Cyprus?" they echoed, disbelieving. "Cyprus?"

"Yes," I mumbled.

"You're going to turn down Cyprus? Do you know how much I'd love a posting to Cyprus?" By now most disbelieving. "You must be mad."

To be honest, I'd been so disappointed about having to leave the Green Jackets that I hadn't really properly considered the posting I'd been given. That evening at dinner my dilemma was discussed openly in the Mess. Everyone offered their advice. Everyone thought I was mad to turn down Cyprus for what they all considered would be a boring alternative. "At least I'd still be with you, still connected to you," was what I wanted to say to them. It was what I thought. I don't think they ever understood the strength of my affection for them.

I don't expect they could ever have understood how unique this feeling of belonging had been to me. It was so special. And, perhaps, as a complete outsider it was stronger and more special to me than they could ever have known. I'd even become very fond of Robert. Since I'd left Battalion HQ and been out of his way in A Company he'd definitely thawed, and if ever I needed some sound advice I always went to him, and I was never let down by his counsel. He thought about things carefully, and seemed to have an innate sense of what was right. With the benefit of hindsight I could now perhaps see why he'd found it difficult to work with me. He was so committed to the battalion, proud to be part of it, and he worked tremendously hard to keep the whole machine running smoothly. I'd arrived completely ignorant. I'd never intended, or wanted, to join the Royal Green Jackets, in fact I'd hardly heard of them when the bombshell had been dropped on me on leaving Sandhurst. (Quite different from the men who decided which regiment or corps they wished to join usually long before they even started training.) It's different for the women now, their future is decided much earlier on in the process, which seems a better and more equal basis. But when I turned up, for poor Robert to deal with, I didn't fit in. I was awkward, often embarrassed, ignorant and quite passive. It must have been intensely irritating for him.

Robert had also fallen in love. His softer side had been discovered, and he was a very happy man. We'd become good enough friends for him to invite me to his wedding, which was a joyous affair. I now looked upon him as a man who deserved to go right to the top of the British Army. Although I couldn't help teasing him occasionally,

"Robert, remember in twenty years time I want an invitation to your knighthood celebrations." And I meant it kindly. If ever I'd had to serve in action I couldn't have wished for a more professional and able commander to serve under than Robert. He'd got what it took.

I spent the next few days mulling things around in my mind. Taking long walks over the beautiful fields. Long swims in the public pool over the road. Chatting to my Sandhurst friends over the net. I'd never been to Cyprus, only on a deckchair to it, so I'd no idea what I'd be missing. Then one of my friends, Bev, rang me to tell me that she'd heard that another female officer, apparently a really lovely fun person, had been posted to the same regiment in Cyprus – 9 Signal Regiment – at the same time. Wow! I'd have another female to talk to, and she'd be as new there as me. I must admit that sounded a bonus. But it still wasn't enough to sway me.

Then, one evening, alone in my room, I was remembering what it was, all that time ago, that brought me into the Army. Actually I was still faintly astonished to be in the Army. I still didn't feel Army, whatever that felt like. And I could still entertain myself as I recalled my transformation from office girl to infantry soldier. I recalled what I'd promised myself then. That this was to be an Experience, an Adventure. Not a life-long career, but something from which to gain the widest possible experience. At that time in my life I was very lost. Unpopular with myself and my family. I had wanted to run as far away from my guilt and my confusion as possible. And I had been very confused. After all I had wanted to fall in love and marry, with a big party, and live happily ever. And having the opportunity within my reach I'd turned it all down. I'd caused distress, turmoil and distrust. Had I paid for it? Was it possible to pay for it? Should I really have had to pay for such a thing? With hindsight I could comfort myself with the fact that if I hadn't turned that marriage down I would never have had these adventures of the last couple of years. And my relationship with my father had been wonderful, full of love and fun once again. I had thirsted for adventure, something that I could always look back on and say,

"OK I didn't do that but I did do That."

I'd joined the army to escape yes, but also to enlarge my world, to increase my experience. So, perhaps the key was there - to stay with 2RGJ would not be to gain the widest possible experience, on the contrary I would be limiting it. Staying on because that was the easy, familiar, thing to do. I had been offered another experience, I must accept change gratefully and open another door. Be glad of the achievements and the friendships I'd made. And move on. I somehow felt that my father would agree that was the right thing to do.

"Don't be afraid of change love. If something's worth doing it's worth doing properly, to the end."

Yes, he'd be proud of me, choosing the difficult path, but the right path. "There's always another day, another way." He'd lived like that. He'd forgiven me because he'd loved me. Oh God, I'll miss you. All of you.

I told the Colonel of my decision the next day. He was kind and wise as always.

"It's the right decision, Gilli" he said in his calm and measured voice. "We'll all be scattering in different directions. Life can't stay the same, better to move on than getting stuck and regretting it. But before you go, and before we all break up, I'm planning to make sure we have a really memorable ending to our tour here. We're going to do something really special in our last week. Something big, something that we'll all remember. There now, you can really enjoy thinking about that!" He laughed wickedly but wouldn't tell me what the "something" was, it was to be a secret, and we all chattered eagerly in the Mess about what sort of brilliant party it might be. It had to be a party didn't it? We had some wonderful fantasies.

A couple of weeks later, with amazingly just one week of our tour left to go, the officers were told to gather in the anteroom of the Mess. It was a 3-line whip, no excuses accepted. We waited in an expectant hush for the Colonel to arrive and as he strode in we all looked up, could this be about our humdinger of a farewell party that he'd arranged for us?

"I said that we would mark the occasion of our breaking up and leaving Warminster. And so we shall." Was he going to tell us he'd booked a really brilliant band, that we'd have fountains of champagne and the best fireworks display this side of the Himalayas?

He continued, "We are all going on an Escape and Evasion Exercise."

There was an awkward silence for a moment or two as we attempted to digest this rather damp news. What about the party? The energy in the room slumped. And then there was a general "Ohhhh nooo," of a response, and a general sinking of shoulders. The Colonel, so delighted with his news, seemed oblivious. He obviously didn't rate farewell parties.

"We are all going up to Newcastle where the Paymaster and the 2ic A company will be dropped on Newcastle Airport roof by helicopter." I stared in horror at Jerry. Dropped on an airport roof? What on earth was coming next?

"Jerry and Gilli will be in disguise as the Mad Professor and his Assistant. Please dress accordingly you two." A general titter went around the room. My mouth was open. I was completely bemused. But Jerry was beaming, this was his sort of stuff.

"The Mad Professor and his Assistant must escape from the airport, and from the rest of the battalion, and get to Kielder Forest by 4-tonne truck. There they must stay in hiding from the rest of the battalion and also from the enemy, the Cambrian Patrol team which will be led by Lieutenant Massingham. Points will be awarded to both the Cambrian Patrol team and the rest of the battalion each time they catch the Professor and his Assistant. We leave tomorrow at 0600 hours. That's all. Thank you." And off he strode.

A buzz of excitement went up around the room. We'd now forgotten about any party. Preparing for tomorrow's departure was going to take all our attention for the next few hours. Jerry and I went into a corner and he, red with mirth, was delighted by my ignorance of escape and evasion tactics. I wished I'd listened more to those lectures we'd had in the "sleeping bag" at Sandhurst. (I've often wished that, actually - having, in a later life, met one of the lecturers again. A most charming man, obviously a world expert in his chosen field, and definitely worth listening to.) However, I'd just have to listen to Jerry and, as had become my tried and trusted way, make the rest up.

The next morning at 0600 hours the battalion waited on the parade square for orders. Jerry and I were to depart sometime after the rest, to give them time to get up North in jeeps and 4-tonne trucks before we were whisked off by helicopter. Time for a last few cups of tea out of real china cups.

It was the oddest experience being in a very busy Newcastle Airport, dressed in strange clothing that we felt would be appropriate for a Mad Professor (actually

Jerry just wore his usual unusual civilian clothes, a long dark cape and a deerstalker hat), and his Assistant, with our rucksacks of rations. We would be in these same clothes for several days, and nights actually, and although it was summer it would be chilly out at night sheltering goodness knew where. We managed to dodge most of the soldiers, weapons in hands, up and down escalators, through departure lounges, restaurants and bars, and eventually back up onto the roof again, scattering startled civilian travellers as we ran. How on earth had they got permission for this? We stayed on the roof for some time basking in the sunshine, and laughing about the absurdity of it all. It was a great game so far, and Jerry was the best company I could have wished for. He simply saw the funny side in everything. After a while, getting uncomfortably hungry, we decided to make our way cautiously off the roof and eventually down to the car park where we knew a 4-tonne truck was waiting to whisk us off to Kielder Forest to hide, hopefully buying a sandwich or six on the way.

This was easier said than done, but thanks to Jerry's panache, and charm, we got out of the airport and into the back of the dark 4-tonne without too much disruption. The journey was short, and we crammed handfuls of delicious sandwiches into our hungry mouths realising that would be the last of the shops, and soon we were unceremoniously bundled out and left in the forest. We decided first that a brew-up was called for and Jerry, unimpressed at my skills with the hexamine blocks, took over. We sipped our hot tea, still laughing at my incompetence, and although we were uncertain of what to do next we felt full of anticipation. It was very quiet just the two of us, seemingly so small sitting under those huge trees.   All we could hear were the birds and the midges.   The latter were just beginning to irritate me, and I started spraying myself all over with the army's best in midge repellent.   I had no reason to doubt its powers at this stage.

"Well come on, can't sit hear all afternoon," surmised Jerry, "better get off."

"Get off where though Jerry?"   I still hadn't got the hang of this yet.

"I don't know do I?"   He laughed.   "We need to set up somewhere to hide don't we?   They'll be looking for us, so we need to cover our tracks."   He started busily covering up the few strands of burnt grass where we'd boiled our water, and I tried to rub out any footprints. Then we ambled off, looking for a cosy hole to set up our safe shelter for the night.   Jerry whistling happily, me trying vainly to swot midges.

We eventually came to a clearing, a small field, and on the edge of this field was a very small, ramshackle hut thing with half a roof made out of rusty corrugated iron.   It all looked very unstable. And most unsavoury.

"Aha," said Jerry, a note of triumph in his voice, "what's this?"

"It's a horrid, filthy little hut," I retorted wrinkling up my nose in disgust, "probably used to be used as a pig sty."

"Mmmm... yes, you're probably right," said Jerry prodding a stick around inside it. "Marvellous.   We'll sleep here tonight."

"What?" I was appalled, "you're not serious?"

"Of course. It provides some shelter. We can put some branches around it. We'll be well-hidden, and quite snug. It'll be a nice pig sty when we've moved in. Home from home. Come on. Let's unpack."

I began to feel rather glum. My skin was beginning to feel clammy and itchy. Inside the pig sty I felt even more dirty, and didn't really want to touch anything. The air felt stuffy and the mixed aromas of peat, rotting leaves, stale goodness-knows-what, and us made me feel a bit creepy. And just what was creeping around in the darkness in here?

"Unpacking" took all of 70 seconds. We were travelling light. At least there were plenty of thick trees for miles around us behind which to be private. Something that had become very high on my priority list. I cheered up a bit. Never mind the pigs, there are lots of lovely trees. And I had Jerry's wonderful sense of humour to keep me entertained. I knew he was a gem amongst men, and if I had to be stuck out here for days I was so very, very lucky to be stuck with him. My stomach ached from endless laughing. It was impossible to remain quiet. How could he continue to be so hilariously witty in these circumstances with just a lump of self-pity for company? We spent much of the evening being rude about each other's talents with the hexamine blocks and fantasising about such luxuries as hot running water and flushing cisterns. But really just something that dealt efficiently with the bloody midges would have done me.

Eventually, after much giggling, crashing about in the woods, falling over several times, with bruises, cracked shins and aching tummy it had to be time to try to get some sleep. I felt somewhat uncomfortable about lying down in that pig sty. Actually putting my head down, even with the ground sheet between me and the earth, was an act of faith. I wasn't too sure what might be running around in the pitch black darkness, and every time I braved closing my eyes they would suddenly open wide again straining to see if anything had crept onto my sleeping bag. I tried so hard not to think of creeping things. And I tried very hard not to think about my incessant itching, all over. I lay still and could hear an owl.

The night was very still, and it felt quite unreal, almost magical to be lying out there, so far away from normal human activity. As on so many other occasions out on exercise I began to feel that I could like it, being so close to nature. It had a strange specialness, almost a mystic quality. Nothing was as wonderful to see and feel as the dawn gathering and spreading. I got to be out in forests and fields all night underneath the twinkling stars. I just would not have ever done this if I hadn't joined the Army. It just wasn't a part of my life. And now, at this very moment, I knew I wouldn't have missed it for the world. I must remember that for the rest of my life. Remember, sometimes, to watch the dawn rising over fields.

Lying there, in our pitch black pig sty, seeing nothing at all seemed to improve my hearing, and I lay there listening to the sounds of the night. Was Jerry asleep? His breathing seemed quite rhythmical now and I didn't want to disturb him. I tried to relax into sleep, but it wouldn't come. Instead I listened to the sounds of the forest again, the owl, the stillness, the crack of a twig.

The crack of another twig. Was that normal? Oh dear, the crack of another twig. That wasn't normal. I lay as still as I could. I didn't dare to breathe. Had they found us?

Jerry's soft little snores began to sound horribly loud. I tried to gently nudge him with my toe through my sleeping bag. If I woke him would he be startled and cry out even louder? Should I just wait? What on earth would happen if they caught us? I felt a bit scared and my throat went dry. It was difficult to keep still. I just knew, could feel even, that they were slowly advancing on our sty. I waited, uncertain of what, if anything, I should do. The hair on my head was tingling. All was very silent.

Suddenly Jerry stirred, and there was a crash as a great black shape forced its way through our attempt at camouflaging the doorway, and we were discovered. There was shouting and confusion. I was rooted to the spot. Then I felt someone grab my arm and Jerry and I were dragged out, somewhat unceremoniously I thought, and triumphantly shown to the rest of the Cambrian Patrol who had our little sty surrounded. They had scored a victory and we were ordered to gather our few bits and were then marched off into the night. We stumbled our way sleepily through the forest at gunpoint. Prisoners for the first time that week. For the life of me I didn't see how we were going to escape, but I'd wait for Jerry to recover his equilibrium and let me in on the plan that I knew would begin brewing in his brain very soon now.

We were caught many times, by both sides, during the week. All they had to do was listen for me laughing at Jerry's wonderful humour which must have echoed loud and clear for miles around. Whenever we managed to escape we had to keep moving on to set up new hide-outs. I got very tired, and began to get quite stroppy when we were, inevitably, disturbed in the middle of the night. I'd found it quite easy in the end to put my head down and shut out all fears of creeping things. I was too tired to care.

But I wasn't too tired to be bothered terribly by the bloody midges. They were the bane of my life. I hated them and even wanted to murder Jerry just by way of a bit of light relief from my mounting and raging frustration. By the final day I'd scratched my face and hands so much that I could see they were beginning to bleed quite badly. Jerry kept shouting at me to stop.

"You'll regret all this scratching, believe me. Just leave yourself alone woman," he demanded time and time again. I became quite miserable and vicious in my attempts to murder horribly any midges I could reach. As I got dirtier I got hotter and stickier, and itchier.

"Good God!" I suddenly exclaimed, as we were trudging wearily along a path on our final day, filthy, bedraggled and tired, "What in God's name is that?"

We began running towards a small building ahead of us. We were breathing hard, excited.

"Lavatories. Public lavatories," breathed Jerry in undisguised delight. "Get in there! Let's make use of them. There might be running water. There might be flushing…….."

We each entered our doorway, thrilled at the prospect of what was undoubtedly before us. The first thing I saw was a small bleary mirror. I stared into it, uncertain of the mess I might see. But I was not prepared for the disfigured sight that stared back at me. I screamed in shock and horror. Tears began to sting my swollen eyes.

"Jerry, Jerry, my face. Why ever didn't you tell me?" I shouted out in great distress, and continued to stare at the swollen, red and blotchy vision that stared back at me from the mirror, and then I dashed back out into the sunlight. "Jerry, why didn't you say?" I was blubbing. Jerry appeared at his doorway, stripped to the waist, his head dripping wet.

"What would you have liked me to say? You look absolutely disgusting and I can't bear to look at you?" I cried even louder now. "Come on old girl," Jerry continued kindly putting his arm around me, "it'll get better, they're only midge bites after all. Perhaps one or two have got a bit infected. I did keep telling you not to keep scratching didn't I?" I was sobbing uncontrollably now. I could now see why my face was so painful as well as itchy. How was I going to face people? Jerry continued, "we go home today remember."

"Yes," I thought, "..home. Everyone will see me. Like this."

"Go and splash some cold water over your face," Jerry continued kindly. "And just remember," he added as I trudged back into the "ladies", "it's more or less all over now."

All over now. Oh God, yes, for me it really was. I'd made my decision and I'd got to stick to it. Our Big Special Farewell Event that we'd all remember was rapidly becoming just that - a memory. As we travelled back to Warminster later that day I felt a deep dread of what I knew I was about to lose. Forever. I yearned for time to stand still, for all of these wonderful people to stay with me, for me to continue to belong to this unique and so very special group. But it didn't happen. Instead it just quietly slipped away.

My last day with the Royal Green Jackets was, on the surface, like any other day. I went out as I had come in. No fuss. I knew this to be their way now. There was a formal dinner in the Mess and my dear band had played "Londonderry Air", and one or two other tunes, especially for me. The Mess staff had tried particularly hard to spoil me, and to cheer me up. I found it very hard to remain unemotional. Impossible, really. I was given pictures and statuettes of riflemen as gifts to treasure always. The Colonel gave a touching farewell speech, and everyone tried not to look at me, so as not to see my brimming eyes.

And I was on my way. There was no longer a place for me here. It was painful that, unlike yesterday, I didn't belong here anymore. Just that one day and the whole of life changes, again. I got into my car and drove off, soggy and tear-stained, past the guardroom and the smart salutes, out of those gates, and out of the world of the Green Jackets forever. I knew it could never be the same again. I knew I could never be the same again. The girl turned infantry soldier. In some ways I felt no different. A bit older, still destined to be single. Sorry Dad. Had I learned more wisdom, or just become more confused? The memories of the lost wedding were no longer so raw, so time had done some healing on that one. But now there was the gap my beloved father had left. When would time heal that? If ever. Time, both the healer and the wounder. I had seen another wonderful world in full colour. Even been a privileged part of it. But now, so suddenly, no longer. Oh such treasured memories. But I had yet another brand new start on a different path. Another door had opened, and I was rushing headlong into it, probably inadequate, certainly a little scared.

What was it he'd said that had spurred me on? "Don't forget, I'll be waiting for the call. Just ring as soon as you get fed up with it and I'll come and get you straight away." Well, he knew me better than anyone.

End

Postscript

Gillian left the army in 1989, after enjoying her Cyprus posting which was, again, completely different to anything she had done before! She then returned to civilian life and, at 38, met a wonderful man and is now happily married with two beautiful children. She went to live in a Hampshire village coincidentally just a few doors down the road from that Great Royal Green Jacket, Field Marshall the Lord Bramall. Try as she might she has still not been able to give up her "searing eyeball pink" lipstick.

Oliver Marchwood also left the Army when his short service commission came to an end, and went on to Captain one of England's great cricket teams.

Jamie McCall-Brown found love and happiness in California, also having left the Army.

Michael MacGowen gave up his career, and just about everything else, and went to work for Mother Theresa in Calcutta.

Robert a very happy family man continues, deservedly, to excel in the Army.